Lore & Legends of Kerala

LORE &
LEGENDS OF
KERALA

SELECTIONS FROM
KOTTARATHIL SANKUNNI'S
Aithihyamala

Translated from Malayalam by
T.C. NARAYAN

Illustrated by
C.N. KARUNAKARAN & NAMBOODIRI

Malayala Manorama

OXFORD
UNIVERSITY PRESS

OXFORD
UNIVERSITY PRESS

Oxford University Press is a department of the University of Oxford.
It furthers the University's objective of excellence in research, scholarship
and education by publishing worldwide in

Oxford New York

Auckland Bangkok Buenos Aires Cape Town Chennai Dar es Salaam Delhi Hong Kong
Istanbul Karachi Kolkata Kuala Lumpur Madrid Melbourne Mexico City Mumbai
Nairobi São Paulo Shanghai Singapore Taipei Tokyo Toronto

Oxford is a registered trade mark of Oxford University Press
in the UK and in certain other countries

Published in India by Oxford University Press
© Oxford University Press 2009

First published 2009
19th impression 2023

ISBN-13: 978-0-19-569889-3
ISBN-10: 0-19-569889-4

Book design by J. Menon, cantocorp.com/design
Printed in India by Repro India Limited, Haryana

Published by Oxford University Press
22 Workspace, 2nd Floor, 1/22 Asaf Ali Road, New Delhi 110002, India

To my mother,
T.C. Janaki Amma,
who gave me life and set its course
and my wife,
Bhavany,
who gave my life its meaning, purpose, and fulfilment

Contents

Acknowledgements

Kerala, successfully branded as "God's own country", draws huge numbers of foreign and Indian tourists. More than two lakhs, nearly ten per cent, of foreign tourists who visit India every year make Kerala their destination. A larger number of domestic tourists are also said to visit Kerala. It is appropriate that *Malayala Manorama* should have decided to promote the wider propagation of at least a selection of the *Aithihyamala* stories and give the tourists something to take back as a valuable reminder of their sojourn in "God's own country".

The credit for the birth and promotion of the *Aithihyamala* series should go to the founder of *Malayala Manorama*, Kandathil Varughese Mappila, who encouraged Kottarathil Sankunni to compile his various articles into a series of books. The ready acceptance and enduring public interest in *Aithihyamala* are reflected in the number of editions published and copies printed since 1909 till as recently as 2003.

For many reasons the translation of a selection of stories from Kottarathil Sankunni's *Aithihyamala* has been a rewarding and challenging task. I was never an ardent student of history. In fact, in my younger days, I viewed history in the same way as one does last year's text books – one learns lessons from them and discards the textbooks themselves. However, there were two women who entered my life, one by divine grace and the other by my choice guided by divine grace. They influenced my life and ensured that my distorted view of history did not become a dogma. It is a coincidence that I am now privileged to translate one of my few concessions to history – *Aithihyamala* – and thereby hangs a tale.

My grandfather had a well-stocked library of English, Malayalam, and Sanskrit books. In my childhood, my mother, herself one of the earliest women post-graduates in Sanskrit from Kerala and Madras University, read out from *Aithihyamala* the stories of miracles, Gods, legendary persons, and elephants as my sister and I listened open-mouthed. Then came the time when I began to read from the *Aithihyamala* as my mother listened. That was my entry into the world of Malayalam literature during the days when those brought up outside Kerala and influenced by teachers from the West considered it fashionable to display a deliberate inability to read, write, or speak Malayalam. I was fortunate in that I was encouraged to do all three as well as read and write Sanskrit, all of which I have nurtured over the years. Then I made a quick foray into K.P. Padmanabha Menon's *History of Kerala* and I did not find history uninteresting. It was perhaps my history textbooks in school and the compulsions of taking examinations that perverted my attitude towards history.

In later years, another woman entered my life and brought with her a passionate love for history. With a remarkable capacity for storage and ability to retrieve, this woman, my wife, regaled me with stories of the courage of the Mewari princesses, the exciting escapades of the European royals and nobles, or even the fun times enjoyed closer to home by our ancestors. Places of historical and tourist interest in India and outside occupied a part of every holiday itinerary and each visit was preceded by intense study. I soon learnt to show visible and audible signs of appreciation as we stood in front of monuments, often badly maintained and broken-down. I got over my dislike for history.

I have spent the last many months going through the arduous process of planning, selecting, structuring, and translating many stories from *Aithihyamala* – and I have done this willingly, happily, and with genuine interest. The full turn of the wheel has been rewarding and satisfying.

To revisit the persons, the elephants, and the temples, and to fall under the spell of miracles and magic and relive my childhood days when I read, and re-read *Aithihyamala* was a fascinating experience. However, to try and reproduce the mystery, the excitement, and the thrills evoked in the original was a testing challenge. Mere translation, however faithful, would not only have not conveyed these emotions but on the other hand, it would have rendered the product "flat" and soulless. I have drawn on all the linguistic resources that I have in order to reflect in English the distinctive flavour and the culture of the periods in which the stories originated. I hope that I have not been unjust to Kottarathil Sankunni and that I have adequately fulfilled the aspirations of the publishers.

I wish to record my appreciation for the willing and splendid support this project has received from the *Malayala Manorama* management with whom this project was launched. Shri K.C. Narayanan, Editor in Charge, *Bhashaposhini*, in particular, deserves a large share of this credit for the efficient manner in which he developed this venture with his characteristic courtesy, patience, and professional wisdom.

Oxford University Press, which is now publishing this book, has brought this project its vast professional experience and its standing for which I owe them my sincere thanks.

My dear friend, Mini Krishnan, is the one person who steered me from being a "bit" writer into writing a major endeavour such as this. She has always espoused the theory that translations rate the same as the original work, as they have to bring in new skill and "technology" to sustain the original flavour of a particular culture in a new language which represents a different culture. Experience tells me that there is much truth in this theory. I was persuaded into translation work by Mini at the most stressful point of my life and this new occupation has not only introduced me to a new skill but has also given me a fresh aim in life.

I cannot afford to forget Jayagovindan Menon who gave us much time, advising and helping with the cover and page design. The Karunakaran and Namboodiri duo has enhanced the impact of the text by their unique illustration styles.

In a major project such as this one there are always more than a few people who play different roles that contribute to its eventual emergence as a complete product. In my case I have been supported by my major asset in life, my network of friends from different walks of life. It is with deep appreciation that I record their assistance and encouragement.

My constant, unobtrusive friend, Maya Jayapal, herself a travel writer of no mean repute, acted as my sounding board on many occasions when I chopped and changed the structure and content of my writing to arrive at an optimum level of satisfaction. Her frank and prompt response was invaluable.

My cousin and close friend, Ranjini Gopinath, became a self-appointed monitor of my project schedule which I took on while still bereft and dazed. She constantly repeated the *"Aithihyamala enthayi?"* mantra (How is Aithihyamala going?), coaxed, nagged, and cheered me out of occasional bouts of hopelessness and purposelessness.

In an effort to get the structure, format, and content of my work right from the foreign readers' perspective, I sent samples of my translation to overseas friends, some of whom had not lived in India. Their feedback as well as that of the official reviewers was invaluable and has been taken into account in the final product.

I cannot but express my gratitude to the friends mentioned below who gave me their time and advice "above and beyond the call of duty": Sir Anthony Hayward, former Chairman of the Shaw Wallace group, my mentor and associate of many years in India and abroad, now retired in the UK, and his family, who have all looked upon India as their second home; Nikki Mohan, travel writer and editor in Eaglemoss Publications in the UK; Glenys Lonsdale, much travelled, formerly of the British High Commission in New Delhi and now a senior corporate executive in the UK; Dr Jonathan Mirsky, prolific writer, noted China expert, former China correspondent of *Observer* and East Asia editor of the *Times*, a former winner of Britain's "International Journalist of the Year" award; and David Wolff who lives in Australia, and is an "India watcher".

I conclude with the hope that this book will truly serve its original purpose and carry the scent and flavour of Kerala beyond the borders of the state, and indeed, of India.

Aithihyamala
A Garland of Legends

Even before the days of European colonization, the Indian sub-continent was a fabled land, reported widely by travellers from Phoenicia, China, Arabia, South East Asia, and Rome. Fantasy mixed headily with reality and some of the latter was even more incredible than the former. Later, the Dutch, the Portuguese, the French, and the British trivialized large parts of our tradition, a defence against complexities they could not fully comprehend or which they did not desire to comprehend. Elephants, fakirs, and magical gems became parts of new tales about India.

All through the centuries of foreign trade and conquest one of the most magnetic regions of the sub-continent has been Kerala, which, with its diverse forms of cultural and natural wealth, cast a romantic and seductive spell over foreigners. The entire content of *"Aithihyamala"* or *"Garland of Legends"* relates to Kerala, that strip of land that lies between the Western Ghats and the Arabian Sea. The compilers and narrators of folklore had two goals – to provide reading pleasure and to highlight personal and social values by describing their successes and the consequences of their failures.

"Aithihya" or "a legendary account" has been an integral part of Indian life from times long past. In fact *"pauranikas"* or those well versed in the Puranas rested their beliefs on three *"pramanas"* or proofs – *Aithihyamanumaanam prathykshamapi* – *aithihyam, anumaanam,* and *prathyaksham,* i.e., legend, inference, and what is visible. It is also relevant to note the origin of the word *"Aithihya"* or *"Ithihasa"*. In Sanskrit *"Ithi"* means "thus" and *"Ha"* stands for "notable", thus indicating the importance given to legendary accounts. Therefore, "Aithihya" has much relevance in providing a link with the past, particularly at a time when old and basic values are being questioned, and history itself is sought to be rewritten.

Aithihyamala has continued to hold the attention of the Malayalam reading public not just from 1909 when the various stories/essays were first published as a book, but from long before when they appeared in the well known Malayalam newspaper *Malayala Manorama* (topping Malayalam readership today) and the monthly *Bhashaposhini*. In the early years of its existence *Aithihyamala* was published by Mangalodayam Company. In 1973 this responsibility was transferred to Kottarathil Sankunni Smaraka Samithi (KS Memorial Society) which had by then been formed. From 1978 and till now Current Books has been publishing reprints every year. The selections and translations in this book are from the sixteenth edition released in 2003.

This is not surprising as this "oldie" has held its sway over generations despite fewer and fewer Malayalis being able to read their own language.

The striking quality of the work of Kottarathil Sankunni is the lesson, statement, or pointer that each story or essay provides on the preservation of basic values of human life. In times gone by, this service was provided by folklore, folk songs, folk art, and so on, but unfortunately, the whole pattern of life has changed and these media themselves have become "endangered species" needing protection. It is essential that the medium of *Aithihyamala* is preserved and given maximum publicity. The range of subjects and regions covered in the eight volumes is staggering – legendary figures, historical luminaries, fables, artistes, famous temple elephants, gods and goddesses, community leaders, and many more. As for the regions, the author undertook painstaking travel through Kerala, those days composed of two princely States and a part of Madras Presidency, at a time when travel facilities were less than basic. He investigated, interacted, and tested with local experts to obtain a reasonably believable and interesting account of the subject. Thereafter he put to work his extraordinary descriptive skill reinforced by the conviction which he displayed in his writing.

Religious faith, respect for elders, reverence for parents and mentors, love for the young, concern for others, compassion, loyalty to dependants, and patriotism are only some of the values which emerge from the huge collection of stories and essays. We live in an age when even these normal values are plugged for mercenary reasons and manipulated to gain less than pragmatic ends. The content of the *Aithihyamala* series displays an even-handed but forceful style of narration which highlights all the above qualities in their purest form.

We live in an age when much is made of our ancient heritage and the need to recapture it. Having said this, attempts are made to revive outmoded ideas which take us back to orthodoxy and prejudices. The contents of *Aithihyamala* are unique in that they are narrations in which the core is easily seen. They can be read for sheer relaxation. The same contents can be studied to provide deep insights into all the human values that we have in our midst and still have difficulty seeing.

It is the ancient culture of Kerala – Kathakali, temple festivals, elephants, religious faiths, martial arts, history, etc. – from which *Aithihyamala* has drawn its inspiration. Where else would one find Ayurveda or indigenous medicine being offered for "running repairs" as part of a tourist package which is lapped up by tourists? Where would you find scores of temple elephants being given annual leave and special medical and nutritional treatment? In the light of this obvious interest it would be distinctly unfair to confine to a tiny section of the reading public this monumental work which will find and deserves an enthusiastic readership not only in India, but outside the country as well.

A Hindu Princess
and Her Islamic Dynasty*

*The story of a Hindu princess who embraced Islam to respect
tradition and started a new dynasty in order to resolve a crisis
with justice, courage, and tolerance.*

Arakkal Beebi's home town was Kannur (formerly Cannanore)
in Chirakkal *taluk* and her family had separated from the local
Chirakkal Kolathiri royal family. This story narrates the events
that led to this separation.

Until the 4th century in the Malayalam era (roughly
13th century AD) the Kolathiri royal family had lived in the
then capital Ezhimalakotta. The growth of the family led to
differences within it and many left the main branch to find
new homes in places such as Katthimangalam, Cherukunnu,
Valapattanam, and so on. The ruler continued to live in the
same palace in Ezhimalakotta. This location is twenty miles
to the north of Kannur and the ruins of this palace are still to
be seen atop the Ezhimala hill. The sea is only a short distance
to the west of Ezhimala. Below the hill was a palatial mansion
with eighteen inner courtyards and a huge area of land around
it. A river flowed past the palace. All around the palace were
several Brahmin homes as well as the residential quarters of
five hundred Nair warriors. Not far away lived wealthy Muslims
who were also courageous soldiers.

One day two young unwed princesses went down to the river to
bathe in their protected bathing place. They spent a lot of time frolicking
in the water, diving and swimming to the middle of the river. After
some time they were tired and the younger of the two princesses swam
back ashore. Her sister was overcome by fatigue and was in danger of
drowning. Seeing this the younger sister cried for help. These cries
were heard by a handsome young Muslim who was bathing just a short

---

*Arakkal Beebi

distance away. He jumped into the water, swam to the princess and pulled her towards the shore. As they approached the shore he found that the princess had stopped in neck-deep water and was refusing to move. Understanding the reason he untied one of the cloths he had around him and threw it to her and then left the place. The princess whose clothes had been washed away in the strong current wrapped the Muslim lad's cloth around herself and went ashore to complete the bath. By this time the maids had rushed in and they escorted the princesses back to the palace.

The news of the rescue spread like wild fire and the ruler, the princess's uncle, was overjoyed. He sent for the Muslim youth who turned out to be one of his soldiers which gave the ruler greater happiness. He rewarded the soldier generously with gifts such as new clothes and a higher rank in the army.

The older princess refused to enter the palace and moved into an outhouse in the palace yard. The elders in the family did their best to persuade her to move back into the palace but she refused. She said that in rescuing her the Muslim youth had held her hand and then given her a cloth which are two acts that constituted the greater part of a marriage ritual. As such a marriage between the princess and a Muslim was not permissible, and the princess argued, she was an outcast and could not enter the palace. Determined to retrieve his young niece at any cost the ruler sent for the local seers and priests to arrange for rituals which would help the princess atone for her perceived misconduct and purify herself. All these wise men saw in this invitation an opportunity to collect much wealth and prescribed lengthy and expensive rituals followed by a lavish feast for all. The ruler was unmoved by this advice and agreed to let them know of the day for the rituals to begin.

The news of the ruler's meeting with the seers and priests reached the princess who remained adamant in her earlier decision. The ruler himself tried and failed to change his niece's decision. Realising the futility of further efforts in this matter it was agreed by all that a palace with all comforts should be built nearby. This was done and the princess was given clothes, ornaments, vessels, and such gifts so that she could continue to live like a princess. In order to ensure her physical security she was given in marriage to the handsome Muslim youth. He was also

given the same privileges as consorts of princesses were entitled to according to the custom of the time. The princess came to be known by the Muslim name "Arakkal Beebi" and her male descendants were referred to as "Arakkal Rajas".

Muslim women are expected to observe *purdah* so that they are protected from the looks of men outside their family. However, in view of the close relationship between the two families, the Arakkal Beebis did not have to follow this custom in their interaction with the men of the royal family. Whenever the members of the Chirakkal Kolathiri family met the Arakkal Rajas the latter always greeted them with traditional gifts. The Arakkal family gradually grew in power and influence and the people coined the slogan "Arakkal is half of Chirakkal".

How did the Arakkal family move to Kannur? In the seventh century of the Malayalam era the Prime Minister of the Kolathiri ruler, Arayankulangara Nayar, embraced Islam and changed his name to Muhammadali but continued as Prime Minister. He also took the ruler's permission to marry one of the Beebis of the Arakkal family. After his days his sons remained to serve the ruler loyally. One of them, Ali Moosa, who was commander of the ruler's army captured the Maldive Islands and presented them to his master. As a reward the ruler presented the Ali Moosa family with eighteen thousand *panam*s (local currency), a fort in Kannur and two villages, Kaanathur and Kaanothuchaal. The ruler soon moved from Ezhumalakotta to Valapattanam and Ali Moosa to Kannur fort.

Ali Moosa then helped the ruler capture Lakshadweep which was duly presented to Arakkal Beebi with an annual tax of six thousand *panam*s to be paid by Lakshadweep. The Kolathiri ruler also gave Ali Moosa the title of Aazhi Raja or "ruler of the seas" which was soon distorted to Ali Raja.

When Malabar became part of British territory Arakkal Beebi handed over the administration of Lakshadweep to the British with the condition that a part of the tax collected should go to her. However, this condition was never honoured and the British treated Lakshadweep as their own territory.

Not so long ago there was a dispute between the British and Ali Raja regarding the administration of Lakshadweep. Finally it ended in a compromise by which the British agreed to make an annual payment of a sizeable sum of money to Arakkal Beebi. Apart from this, the entire Chirakkal family was also awarded a privy purse. The Arakkal and Chirakkal families continue to live in amity to this day and may God help them to remain so with greater happiness and prosperity.

The Arithmetic of Faith*

*The story of how faith saved the day
and how a temple commemorates the event.*

What is now known as Thiruvalla in Central Travancore was in the olden days named Mallikavanam or Jasmine Forest (*mallika* – jasmine, *vanam* – forest). It was a prosperous area with nearly three thousand wealthy Brahmin families resident. One of the families was "Sankaramangalath" which over time came to be abbreviated to "Chankroth". This family was childless and consisted of Narayana Bhattathiri and his wife Sridevi, known as Chankrothamma or the "matriarch of Chankroth". Serving them was their maid also known as Sridevi but true to the custom of those days was called differently by the name Chiruthechi. Her son Mukundan was also living with them and he was called Kunnan.

Bhattathiri was a devotee of Lord Vishnu and was known for his generosity and fine character. His wife Sridevi was no different and both of them spent their days in prayer and the observance of religious rituals. *Dashami* or the tenth day of the lunar cycle permitted only one meal, *Ekadashi* or the eleventh day demanded prayer without sleep and food, and *Dwadashi* or the twelfth required that as many *brahmachari*s or unmarried Brahmins as possible should be fed before the two of them had their only meal of that day. Despite their life of devotion to their Lord, Bhattathiri died leaving the family childless. However, this did not alter the lives of Sridevi and her servants.

Sridevi was not literate and soon had difficulty identifying the right days for her rituals. She depended on others for the correct information and finally decided to devise her own method of estimating the right days for various rituals. Starting with one of the eleventh days she placed a pebble in a vessel every day and when the pebbles numbered

---

*Chankrothamma

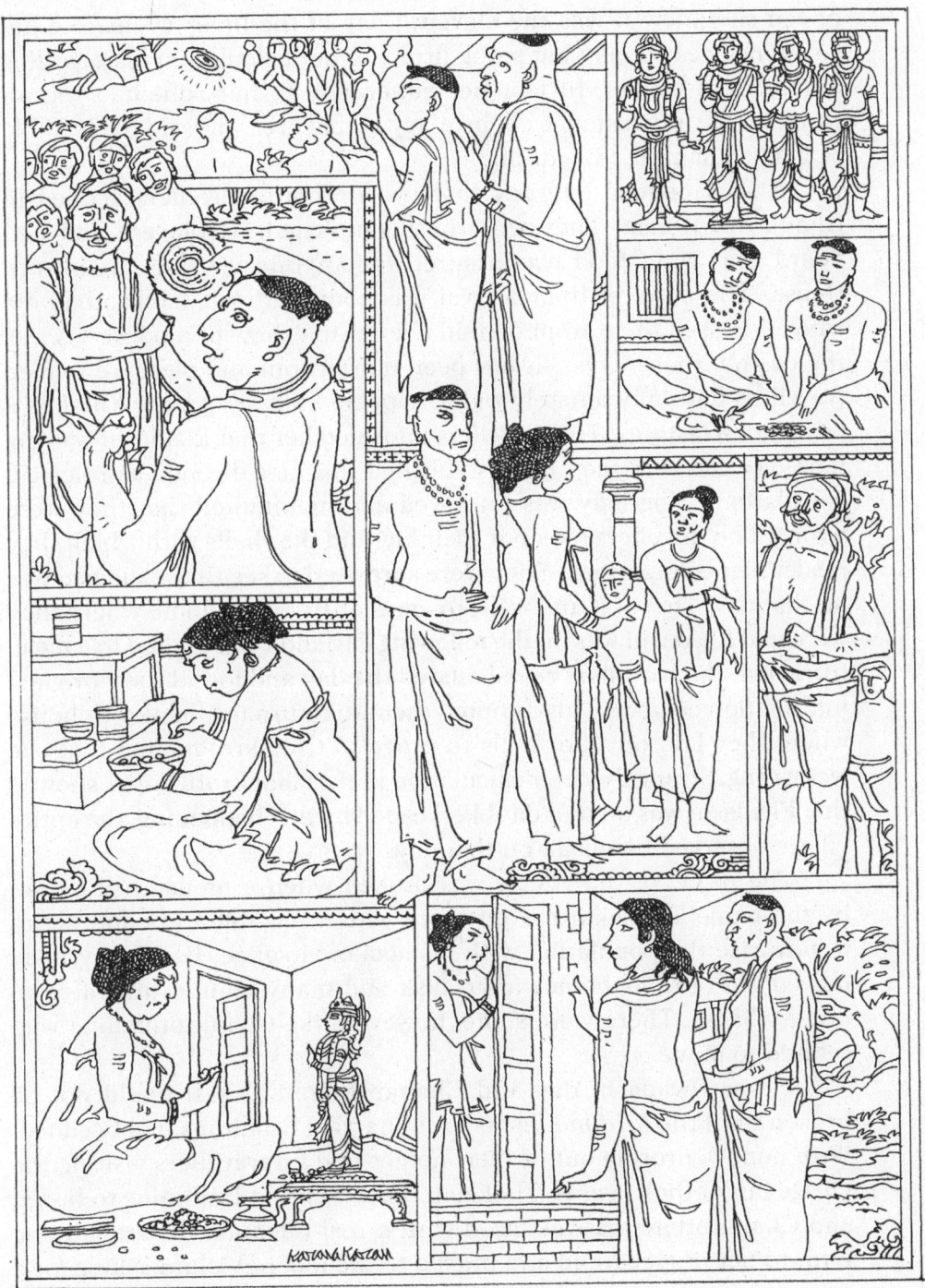

fifteen she knew it was the eleventh day of the lunar cycle. She did go wrong occasionally but stuck firmly to her calculation disregarding advice from others. In fact her adherence to her schedule was so resolute that any instance of obstinacy in that area was said to resemble "Chankrothamma's Ekadashi"!

It so happened one day that two Brahmin travellers arrived in Chankroth House. They were both renowned astrologers and had heard that good food was assured for anyone visiting Chankroth House. The news of their arrival was conveyed to Chankrothamma who addressed them from behind a door in a show of modesty as was the custom those days. "It has been our custom and pleasure to feed travellers but unfortunately today happens to be Ekadashi which is a day of total fasting." The travellers informed her that Ekadashi was the next day and that they had established this fact through astrological calculations. The lady was unmoved and maintained that they were wrong. The travellers took out their bag and the shells with which they made their calculations. They were surprised to see that Ekadashi was on that day. They left and went to another Brahmin home where they were told Ekadashi was on the following day and were invited to a meal. Intrigued, the travellers re-calculated the day and found their original information correct. This tempted them to return to Chankroth house where they laid out the shells to prove to Chankrothamma that she was wrong. Strangely, their calculation in the Chankroth house showed that Ekadashi was on that day! Persuaded by this happening, the entire village observed Ekadashi on that day.

The peace of the village was broken when a monster of a man by the name Thokalan moved there with a few followers and began to terrorise the population with his acts of violence. Hardly anybody moved out of their homes after dusk and many families migrated to other villages. There were some, however, like Chankrothamma who refused to move.

It was Dwadashi day and Chankrothamma's fast could not be broken until the *brahmacharis* or unmarried Brahmins had been fed. With none venturing out of their homes and no travellers visiting the village out of their fear of Thokalan there were no Brahmins to be fed and Chankrothamma was faced with a real dilemma. In despair she went to her prayer-room and prayed to the idol of Vishnu asking for a solution. In a short time there was a cry from outside asking if there was food available. Chankrothamma saw a young Brahmin outside the house holding a staff and asked him to have a quick bath in the pond nearby and return for his meal. The young man insisted on a bath in the river and was unmoved by his hostess's warnings about Thokalan. He left for the river and was inevitably waylaid by Thokalan. A fight followed in which the Brahmin's staff suddenly turned into a *chakra*—one of Lord Vishnu's weapons, the divine discus Sudarshana—which beheaded Thokalan. His cries attracted his followers who came running only to meet the same fate as their leader. The discus transformed back into a staff as soon as it was washed clean in the river.

Chankrothamma was worried at the delay in the Brahmin's return and was overjoyed when he came back accompanied by five other young friends. The news of Thokalan's death at the hands of a young Brahmin spread like wild fire and crowds gathered outside Chankroth house shouting their request to see the discus which slew Thokalan and restored peace to the village. The discus made its appearance in all its glowing splendour and the spot where it appeared became the location of a temple devoted to the Lord Vishnu's discus, Sudarshana. Chankrothamma surrendered all her property to the temple and designated Brahmin families for the management of the rituals therein. The young Brahmin asked the people to treat Sudarshana with reverence so that they could prosper and flourish. The crowds stood with their eyes closed in prayer and when they opened their eyes they found that the Brahmins had disappeared and with them, Chankrothamma, and her constant companion and maid Chiruthechi as well. That village came to be known as Chakrapura because of the presence of the chakra or the discus. With the setting up of a Shri Vallabha temple the whole area was referred to as Srivallabhapura which in time was distorted to what is now called Thiruvalla.

The Arithmetic of Faith

From Poverty to Royalty*

*The story of the rise of a family from poverty
to royalty and its eventual decline.*

Long ago in Kumaranallur in the old Travancore State there
was a Nambudiri family by name of Chempakasseri. In that
poverty-stricken family there was no adult male but only a
young widow and her young son who was learning the Hindu
scriptures. One day in the afternoon over five hundred armed
strangers appeared in Kumaranallur. They were defeated
soldiers fleeing from the war between the rulers of Cochin
and Calicut. They had not eaten for two or three days and
were famished. They came across a few young Nambudiri
men, explained their sorry state and asked where they could
hope to get a meal. Some of them ignored the soldiers while
a few others pointed at the poor Chempakasseri lad following
them and said sarcastically, "Ask him as he may be able to
find you a meal. He is a very wealthy man." The soldiers took
this advice seriously and approached the embarrassed young
man to ask for help. He knew that the others had done this
maliciously to insult him. He took off a gold chain from around
his neck and gave it to the soldiers suggesting that they could sell it
and make arrangements for a meal. He added that they should see
him after their lunch.

The soldiers enjoyed their lunch and in seeking directions to the
Chempakasseri home discovered that the family was a very poor one.
They went there and said to their benefactor, "Please tell us what you
wish us to do for you for we are from now on yours to command." The
young man was touched by this and he replied, "If that is what you wish
so be it. However, you must know that I have nothing in my possession
with which to feed you or even feed myself. So the first task is to find
food for all of us. I suggest you go to the homes of the boys who wickedly

---

*Chempakasseri Raja

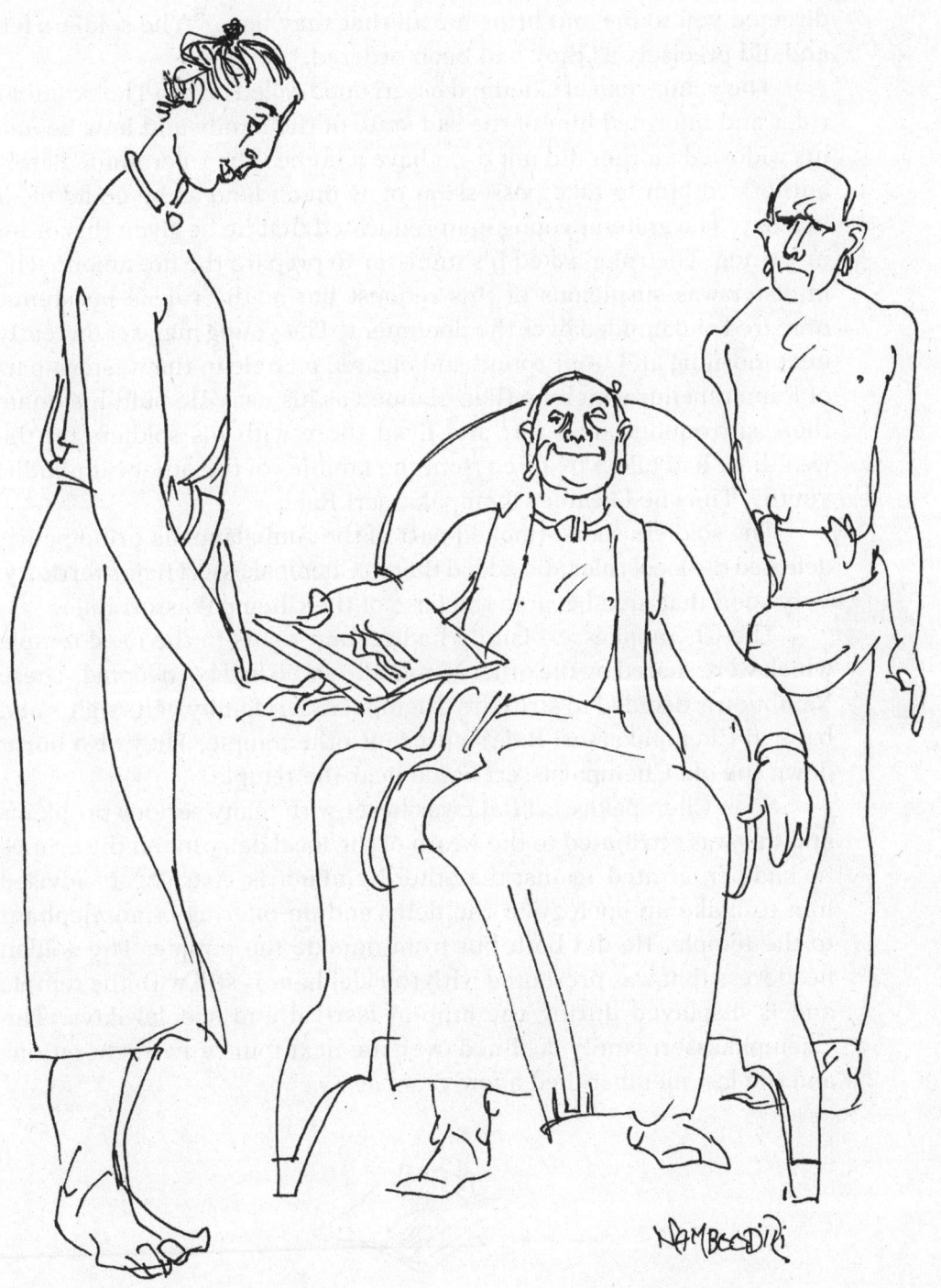

directed you to me and bring me all that they have." The soldiers left and did precisely as they had been ordered.

The young man of Chempakasseri once called on the Thekkumkur ruler and informed him of the sad state of the family and how he and his widowed mother did not even have a home. The ruler immediately authorized him to take possession of as much land as he could clear in a day. The grateful young man requested that he be given this order in writing. The ruler asked his minister to prepare the document. The minister was suspicious of this request but at the ruler's insistence prepared and handed over the document. The young man set out early next morning and went round and cleared a circle in the western part of Kumaranallur which he then claimed as his own. He built his home there surrounded by a fort and lived there with his soldiers on the wealth he had taken by force from the families of the other Nambudiri youths. Thus he became Chempakasseri Raja.

The soldiers soon attacked part of the Ambalapuzha principality, defeated the local ruler and added that to Chempakasseri Raja's territory. Very soon that area became the base of the Chempakasseri Raja.

The Chempakasseri family had certain rights in the local temple which were shared by the other Nambudiris who had been looted. These Nambudiris decided to strip the Chempakasseri family of its rights and banned Chempakasseri Raja's entry into the temple. They also burnt down the old Chempakasseri home near the temple.

Soon Chempakasseri Raja was beset with many serious problems and this was attributed to the wrath of the local deity for all the crimes he had perpetrated against the other Nambudiris. Astrologers advised him to make an apology to the deity and an offering of an elephant to the temple. He did both but from outside the temple. The golden headdress that was presented with the elephant is still with the temple and is displayed during the annual festival and special days. The Chempakasseri family declined over the next four or five generations and the last member died a few years ago.

Snake Power*

How a chance meeting with a divine visitor led a poverty-stricken family to a position of power and vast influence.

 Long ago there lived in the erstwhile Cochin State a Nambudiri family, religious, well-versed in Hindu scriptures but in straitened financial circumstances. The depth of their poverty became so acute that a senior of the family went to the famous Tiruvanjikulam temple to pray to the deity for relief from their many problems. The Nambudiri's stay in the temple was nearing twelve years when, late at night, he went to the temple pond to collect some water. There, standing by the side of the pond, was a man with a divine bearing. The Nambudiri asked him who he was to which the man responded, "Why do you wish to know all this? Please collect your water and leave." As the Nambudiri stood there wondering who this strange man could be he saw something in the man's hand glowing like a burning ember. The Nambudiri asked the man what it was and the man replied with a question, "Have you seen a diamond?" When the Nambudiri said he had not the man said, "I shall give it to you but you must give it back after you have looked at it." The Nambudiri took the diamond and looked at it but he then wished to show it to the Raja of nearby Kodungallur who was a friend.

He asked the man if he could take it to the Raja, show it to him and come straight back to return it. The man agreed saying he could not wait too long and that the Nambudiri would have to hurry. The Nambudiri left with the diamond and when the Raja saw it he was very reluctant to return it saying he was willing to buy it at any price. The Nambudiri refused to break his promise to the owner of the diamond, insisted on taking it from the Raja and finally restored it to the man near the pond. The man promptly disappeared leaving the Nambudiri blinded by the brightness of the diamond and dazed by the whole strange experience.

---

*Paambu Mekkattu Nambudiri

It took a while for him to recover from both after which he collected water from the pond and left.

The Nambudiri could not sleep that night and lay wondering whether he could have persisted with his questions to find out who the man was. After a while he drifted into sleep but woke up very soon. He saw the moonlight and thinking he had overslept, rose and made straight for the pond to commence his daily ablutions. There he saw a man and asked who he was. The reply was as unhelpful as it was before, "Why do you wish to know this? It is too early for your bath and you may go back and sleep." Realising that this person was the same one he had seen before, the Nambudiri prostrated before him and pleaded with him to reveal his identity. The person then revealed that he was Vasuki, the king of serpents. Then the Nambudiri requested him to show him his real form. Vasuki declined saying that this would fill the Nambudiri with fear but when the latter insisted, Vasuki obliged but in a size as small as the ring on Lord Shiva's finger. Even this was so frightening that the Nambudiri fell into a faint and did not wake up for quite some time. When he did finally wake up Vasuki asked him if he wished to ask him for anything. The Nambudiri replied, "I wish to have your constant presence in my home. Please find me some relief from my utter poverty. I want nothing else." Vasuki agreed and said, "So be it. You will finish your twelve years of worship in two or three days' time after which you may go back home. By then I shall also be there having taken my Lord's permission. I shall then fulfil your desires. You may now have your bath." Vasuki thereafter disappeared.

The Nambudiri concluded his worship and returned home. He put away his palmyra thatched umbrella in the eastern verandah and went to bathe and complete his rituals. When he came back he was taken aback on seeing a snake on his umbrella. This snake turned into that divine form which then addressed the Nambudiri, "Do not fear for it is me, Vasuki. My Lord Shiva is pleased with your honesty and devotion. He has sent me here to fulfil your desires. Here is the diamond that you saw when we first met. Please store it here with great care for there will be no poverty where it rests. One more serpent, a *naga yakshi*, a divine serpent in feminine form, will be joining me here soon and there is no cause for fear."

At this time the matriarch of the Nambudiri family arrived on the scene. As soon as she put her umbrella down a snake decended from it and turned into a stunningly beautiful woman who went and stood by Vasuki's side. Vasuki then spoke, "Please establish likenesses of ours at this spot and worship them without fail as your family deities. This will give you continued prosperity. Many serpents will make your property their home. Please treat them as members of this family. The property is to be treated as sacred and should not be defiled in any way. There must be a place allocated for each natural function and strictly used as such. The yard should never be dug or disturbed and fires should not be lit anywhere outside. There must be another small building on the next plot of land to be used for activities connected with birth and death, and for isolating womenfolk during their monthly cycles. Serpents may be seen inside and outside the house but have no fear as they will not harm any member of the family. Their venom will not affect anyone in the family. Any snakebite victims from outside may not be treated by your family but diseases arising out of the curse of serpents may be cured. Two lamps must be lit and tended without a break where our idols are established. The soot and the oil of the lamps can be used by your family to cure skin diseases resulting from the curse of the snakes. You may ensure that all that I have said is passed on to the others in the family and to the following generation." Vasuki and his companion then disappeared.

The Nambudiri followed Vasuki's instructions scrupulously. Vasuki and his companion were installed in the eastern verandah and accepted as the family deity. The original family name changed from "Mekkattu" to "Paambu Mekkattu", "*paambu*" meaning "snake", and to this day that is the name by which the family is known. The fortunes of the family changed with many people coming to worship the deities and seeking relief from diseases resulting from the curse of the snakes. The fame of the family and stories of its success in curing certain types of ailments spread far and wide. Offerings for the worship and the cure brought prosperity to the family. It also became a practice every year to have special worship rituals for the deities for forty-one days from the first day of the Malayalam month of *Vrischokom* (October/November). A Pandya king sought help from the Paambu Mekkattu family for curing a leprosy-like disease which had resisted all treatment. The Nambudiri cured the king fully and, needless to say, was generously rewarded.

On their way back from their visit to the Pandya king the Nambudiri family was approaching the town now known as Nagercoil, then in South Travancore (now in Tamil Nadu), when they heard the cries of a woman from within the nearby forest. On finding the woman she said she was cutting grass when her sickle hit a stone idol hidden in the grass. The idol began to bleed and this was continuing unchecked. The Nambudiri searched in the dense grass and found the idol of a serpent with five heads and one of the heads was still bleeding. The Nambudiri stopped the bleeding using his spiritual power and with the help of a few local people procured the material for a ritual which was promptly conducted. The woman was sent away suitably consoled. Thereafter the Nambudiri mobilised the local population and convinced them that if they commenced worship of the newly-found snake idol the snake god would bless them all with prosperity. He also had the area cleared at his expense and a shelter built to protect the idol from the weather. That was the origin of the name of the town "Nagercoil" or "Temple of the Nagas (snakes)". Thanks to the involvement of "Paambu Mekkattu" Nambudiri the temple became well-known, devotees came in large numbers from near and far, and the area became prosperous as a result. With this the Nambudiri family also became wealthier.

The temple in Nagercoil is slightly below ground level and the soil around it is damp while that in its proximity is totally dry. The soil around the idol is red in colour and this is attributed to the bleeding from the head of the idol. Devotees who visit the temple take back a small quantity of the red soil and use it for curing skin ailments. Despite the quantity of red soil that is removed by the devotees, the level of this soil around the idol has not fallen. After a time the Nambudiri wished to have a permanent temple built and arrangements were made to start this work. However, on the night before the work was to commence the idol appeared in a dream and expressed his desire that no change should be made to the temple. The plan to build the new temple was abandoned.

"Paambu Mekkattu" Nambudiri continued to take an active part in the affairs of the Nagercoil temple till old age made this difficult. His sons and grandsons took over these duties and eventually limited their responsibility to participating in the annual ten-day festival in the Malayalam month of Meenam (February/March). Soon the Travancore government assumed the management of the temple but continued the practice of "Paambu Mekkattu" Nambudiris performing the rituals during the festival, for which they were given a remuneration.

There was once in the "Paambu Mekkattu" family a Nambudiri who did not much care for old customs and traditions. He decided to celebrate an event in the main house which violated the original agreement with the serpent-king, Vasuki. While digging in the compound to erect some posts for the *pandal* or marquee, the workers came across snakes' nests. Some of the eggs were broken and a few snakes had also died. Very soon the entire property was infested by serpents and the residents were terrified. Astrologers were consulted and it was only after the prescribed rituals were conducted in atonement that the serpents withdrew.

The "Paambu Mekkattu" family had the sole right to handle all rituals connected with *sarpa kavu* or snake temples but the number of these temples increased. This task was then assigned to nominees.

The serpents were the family deities and also the guardians of the "Paambu Mekkattu" family. Not a piece of the family possessions could be taken out of the house. The notorious dacoit Chekannan once decided to break into "Paambu Mekkattu" house on his way back from a burglary. He and his men put down their stolen possessions in order to steal money and ornaments from "Paambu Mekkattu" house. When they returned to collect their original loot they found a serpent, coiled, hood spread, on each of the bundles. When they tried to leave, their paths were blocked by more serpents. They stood there till dawn till one of the family woke up. The gang fell at his feet and pleaded for forgiveness after which the serpents disappeared.

One of the "Paambu Mekkattu" Nambudiris was on his way to Nagercoil when he stopped for the night in the Ambalapuzha temple. That night he was proceeding towards the temple tank when he accidentally stepped on a snake which promptly bit him. He knew the bite would not affect him but that the snake would die unless the venom was removed from it, for that was what Vasuki had said long before then. He sent for the temple authorities and asked for three flat, open vessels, milk, and two tender coconuts. He put milk in one vessel, tender coconut water in the second and plain water in the third. He ordered the snake to get into the milk which it did with great difficulty and the milk turned dark. Then the snake entered the coconut water which also turned black. Thereafter it was asked to bathe in the pure water and leave. Thus the life of the snake was saved.

The senior most "Paambu Mekkattu" Nambudiri happened to visit the Vayaskara family. The head of that family asked whether the snake temple near their pond could be moved elsewhere. The trees around the temple were shedding leaves and spoiling the water in the pond and they did not wish to cut the trees as they were near the temple. The Nambudiri said he could do that but in return asked that the pond be moved elsewhere too. When the Vayaskara senior pleaded inability to do this the Nambudiri said, "Well, in that case let the temple stay where it is. Please consider that snakes are like us and prefer to stay in familiar surroundings. These snakes have always lived by the side of the pond and may not wish to move."

There are several stories about the relationship between the "Paambu Mekkattu" family and the snakes and how they looked after each other's interests. The above are only a few of them to illustrate this relationship.

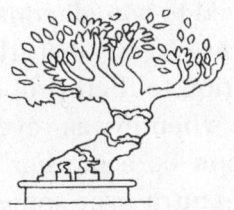

Born to Win*

*How intellectual rivalry led to the breeding of
a genius to ensure victory.*

Every year the ruler Mana Vikraman of Kozhikode (erstwhile Calicut) used to host a convention of Brahmins learned in the Vedas and other scriptures. The venue was the local Thali temple. Included in the programme was a series of debates for which cash rewards were given to the winners. There were one hundred and eight prizes and the one hundred and ninth was for the oldest participant.

In course of time it so happened that the numbers of scholars among the local Brahmins declined and Brahmins from other parts of the country began to participate. For a period the prizes were shared by local and outside Brahmins till a time came when all prizes went to the visitors.

It so happened that a scholarly Brahmin named Uddandan came from outside to take part in the debate. He was a brilliant poet skilled in debate. He was arrogant and made his entry into Kozhikode reciting his own Sanskrit verse which likened the local scholars to elephants in the *Vedanta* forest and asked them to flee to make way for the Uddanda lion. Uddandan won all the debates and the prizes. The ruler was very pleased with Uddandan's skills and persuaded him to stay back in the palace. Uddandan continued to win all contests year after year.

The local Brahmins were greatly disturbed by their lack of success and decided to find a solution to their problem. For this purpose they met in Guruvayur temple when it was revealed that a lady in a local Brahmin family would soon be a mother. This gave them an idea. They recited a powerful mantra over some butter and gave it to the pregnant lady asking her to have it every day till the baby was born. They themselves spent their time praying to the Guruvayur deity with great fervour. In course of time, thanks to the power of prayer and divine blessing, a baby boy was born to the lady.

---

*Kaakkasseri Bhattathiri

The baby displayed great intelligence throughout his infancy and childhood. When he was three his father died and he had to perform the rites. The rites included feeding the crows and the little boy could identify the crows which came or did not come each day. Thus he came to be known as "Kaakkasseri Bhattathiri", "kaakka" meaning "crow" and Bhattathiri denoting the exalted status of his community.

The sacred thread ceremony of Brahmin boys is usually held when they are eight years old after which they commence their education in rituals and scriptures. The hero of our story had his first language lesson when he was three and his thread ceremony when he was five-and-a-half. He had no difficulty in his studies and displayed great intellectual brilliance. By the time he was a youth he had mastered the scriptures and was able to discuss them. The local Brahmins decided that the time was ripe for him to participate in the annual convention. The proposal was put to young Bhattathiri who readily agreed.

It was Uddandan's habit to take his parrot with him to the convention and place it in front of him. This parrot was an expert in debating and often acted as Uddandan's spokesman. Bhattathiri knew about this and asked his servant to accompany him with a cat. When all including the ruler had assembled, the servant handed the cat to Bhattathiri and withdrew.

The ruler saw this young man and asked if he had come to join the contest. Bhattathiri replied affirmatively whereupon Uddandan made a remark in Sanskrit about Bhattathiri's small frame. Bhattathiri responded in Sanskrit promptly parrying this comment and re-structuring Uddandan's own comment to turn the tables on him. Uddandan was embarrassed.

It was time for the debate to start and Uddandan moved his parrot to the front. Bhattathiri did the same with his cat. On seeing the cat the parrot lost its voice! Uddandan himself had to debate and as the intensity of the debate grew it became obvious that Bhattathiri could not be challenged. The ruler put an end to the debate and said that the winner of the contest would be the one who could give the most interpretations of the first verse of the famous Sanskrit composition *Raghuvamsha*. This was done on the assumption that Uddandan was the undisputed scholar in this area. Uddandan gave four detailed interpretations and the entire assembly saw that it would be difficult to beat his performance. Bhattathiri amazed everybody by interpreting the verse in eight different forms and Uddandan himself conceded defeat. The one hundred and eight prizes were won by Bhattathiri. Uddandan then claimed that the prize for the oldest must go to him. Bhattathiri challenged this saying that if age in years was the criterion his servant aged eighty-five would be the winner. If on the other hand "oldest" meant "maturity of knowledge" then he himself would be the winner. The one hundred and ninth prize also went to Bhattathiri. When the convention dispersed the visiting Brahmins left greatly chastened and the local ones much delighted. Bhattathiri and Uddandan met several times thereafter in the ruler's annual and other contests and Bhattathiri remained unbeaten.

By the time Bhattathiri became an adult his brilliance and scholarship were incredible. He then went on his travels to far off places. He happened to reach and rest in a wayside place where many travellers of different communities were staying. Two factions among them had a disagreement which grew into a violent conflict. One of the sides went to the authorities and complained and both sides were then summoned for a hearing. When they had recited their separate grievances they were asked if there were witnesses to the incident. Bhattathiri was cited and summoned. He was asked if he could give details of the conversation that ignited the fight. Bhattathiri explained the circumstances and then said that as different languages were spoken and he did not know them he could only repeat the conversation as he had heard it. Then he gave the authorities a verbatim account of the entire conversation which he had heard and absorbed but did not understand! His power of retention was phenomenal.

Bhattathiri did not believe in the superiority and inferiority of communities, untouchability, and so on. He would mix with anybody, eat anywhere. He considered a bath as a necessity imposed by considerations of hygiene rather than as a means of purification. All this worried the local Brahmins seriously but no one had the courage to tell him that these practices had made him an outcast.

At the end of one of the annual conventions when, as usual, Bhattathiri won all the prizes the Brahmins had a dialogue with him. Without alluding to the real purpose of the conversation they asked him what one should do to ward off danger. He replied that they should remember the lotus feet of the Devi. Their next question was what would happen as a result. He said that the thought of the lotus feet had the power to subdue even the gods. Bhattathiri did not realize that he was the "danger" they were referring to.

The worship of Devi started promptly the next day with powerful verses being recited and many rituals performed. These went on for forty days and on the forty-first day Bhattathiri appeared asking for some water to drink. He stood outside, drank the water, and put down the vessel upside down as prescribed for outcasts. He then admitted he was an outcast and promptly left. He was never seen again.

The Martial Arts Teacher*

*How martial arts were popular among ordinary
people and royalty alike in ancient Kerala.*

Once upon a time there was a Brahmin who wished to learn the local system of martial arts. He sought an audience with the third prince of Kozhikode (erstwhile Calicut) who was an expert and requested him to take him as a disciple. The prince agreed and the training commenced at an auspicious hour.

After a year's rigorous training the prince asked his disciple, "How many men can you defend yourself against?" When the confident reply was "Ten thousand," the disciple was advised to continue his training. The prince asked the same question at regular intervals and the replies were different. The defensive capability claimed by the disciple declined each time by half, and each time the prince informed his disciple that his training was not complete. At the end of twelve years, the disciple conceded he could defend himself only against one man. His training did not end there but continued further until the Brahmin became well-versed in defensive and offensive skills. The objective was to train until "the whole body became the eye". Then came the surprise test when he was ambushed by two soldiers with their spears as he was on his way to bathe, liberally covered in oil. He dodged the attack skilfully and only then did the prince agree that the training had ended. The teacher and disciple parted company after the latter had made the traditional offerings to the teacher and received his blessings.

In the course of the Brahmin's travels he spent a short time in Kayamkulam training the local ruler's army. Thereafter he reached Padmanabhapuram on the outskirts of Thiruvananthapuram (erstwhile

---

*Kallanthattil Gurukkal

Trivandrum) where Maharaja Marthanda Varma of Travancore was in residence. He sent word to the Maharaja introducing himself and requesting an audience. The Maharaja was looking for a teacher of martial arts for his nephew Rama Varma and had failed to find a suitable one. The Brahmin was asked to present himself before the ruler at noon the next day inside the "walled city". When he reached the gate the next day, armed with his sword and shield, he found all the four gates locked and knew he was being tested. He decided to use his acrobatic skills and took a flying leap over the wall. In the short moment that he was in the air over the wall he saw that the landing space inside the wall was planted with high, sharp spikes. In a flash he decided to land on the spikes on his shield which he did safely. He then leapt back over the wall and was about to go back leaving word that he found all gates locked. The Maharaja who was hiding near the gate emerged and assured the Brahmin that he would indeed be the new teacher.

Following his appointment as a "*rajaguru*" or "teacher of the royal family", the Brahmin was given the title of "Gurukkal" or "revered teacher" as well as property free of all taxes. He then came to be known as "Kallanthattil Gurukkal", Kallanthattil being his original family name.

When the Maharaja moved permanently to Thiruvananthapuram the Brahmin also moved with him where he was given a new house. In course of time his family joined him setting up their base in Thiruvalla, not far from Thiruvananthapuram, while he continued his successful term in Thiruvananthapuram, receiving more acclaim and benefits from the ruler. The Kallanthattil family continues to flourish and by tradition, even today the ruler makes an offering to the "Gurukkal" on the concluding day of the Puja or Navarathri festival every year. Although the royal family does not train in martial arts these days, the traditional role of the Gurukkal is still with the Kallanthattil family.

There are many stories about the Gurukkal's disciples and of Rama Varma of Travancore in particular. When he was Maharaja, he used to invite a large number of Brahmins to participate in an important ritual held irregularly. This number included many Brahmins who had received training in the martial arts from various teachers.

One of them known as "Mundiyoor" had smeared himself liberally with oil and, clad only in a loin-cloth, was on his way to the nearby pond for a bath. On the way he came across an old Nair carrying a pot of ghee on his head and a stout stick under his arm. Mundiyoor asked the Nair for the stick. The conversation that followed went like this:

Nair: Why do you need a stick? A stick is for an old man.

Mundiyoor: You can get another one.

Nair: So can you!

Mundiyoor: If you don't give me the stick I shall have to take it by force.

Nair: Oh, I would like to see you do that.

Mundiyoor went to the Nair and tried to pull the stick from under his arm. When he failed, he tugged with both hands but without success. When he persisted in harassing the Nair, the latter made a quick twist and turned his body to the right side. Mundiyoor suddenly discovered that his grip on the stick was stuck and he could not let go. The Nair walked fast with Mundiyoor following him covered in oil and wearing nothing but a loin-cloth. The Nair went to the venue of the ritual and waited there for his turn to measure and deliver the ghee. While all this was being done, Mundiyoor was forced to wait in the sun in his loin-cloth and coated with oil. The news reached the Maharaja who sent for them.

The Maharaja asked Mundiyoor why he was in this strange predicament. Mundiyoor burst into tears overcome by shame that a trained young man like him had been so easily put in his place by a much older man. The ruler ordered the Nair to free Mundiyoor which the Nair did by reversing his twist and the turn.

Rama Varma recognized the complicated manouvre used by the Nair to trap Mundiyoor and it also struck him that he may have met the Nair before. On enquiring about his identity, the Nair said in all humility, "I am one of Your Highness's tenants and have come to deliver some ghee for the ritual." When the Maharaja asked him specifically about their prior meeting the Nair continued, "When Your Highness attacked Kayamkulam I was one of the Kayamkulam Raja's soldiers. When Your Highness jumped over the city wall on horseback I was the one who wounded the horse with my sword. The horse fell outside the wall and Your Highness jumped into the city." Rama Varma remembered this incident well and was very pleased indeed to know that the Nair was also a disciple of his own Kallanthattil Gurukkal during the latter's short term with the Kayamkulam ruler.

The visiting Brahmins trained in martial arts were all invited to a trial of strength in the presence of the Maharaja. Mundiyoor was among the invitees. An oval-shaped iron ingot was placed in the arena and by turn the participants were asked to move it from where it was. Almost all of them failed to even lift it. Mundiyoor managed to lift it knee-high. The Nair raised it waist high. The Maharaja himself then entered the arena and said, "I am old and weak now but I shall try." He lifted it up to the height of his neck and then revealed that it was his practice in his youth to lift the ingot hundreds of times and toss it back over his head! The Nair was rewarded with a tenancy free of all dues and with a monthly remuneration.

As for Rama Varma himself, he was severely tested by his uncle Marthanda Varma after his training. The Maharaja hid himself behind a staircase as the prince was on his way up and suddenly attacked the prince with his sword. The prince instinctively ducked and the sword cut down a rafter from the roof. The Gurukkal appeared on the scene and demanded of the Maharaja the reason for this unprovoked attack. The Maharaja replied, "I wished to test my nephew to check if he had benefited from his training. He is of no use to me if he cannot even defend himself and, of course, if he can defend himself no harm would come to him from the attack." It was after several such tests that Rama Varma was allowed to accompany his uncle on his military expeditions and later conduct them on his own.

Kandankoran of Kitangoor*

*Can a trained elephant be left free to live and move as he wishes?
Kandankoran was proof that it could and that
such trust would not be betrayed.*

In Travancore State there was a famous temple in Kitangoor in Ettumanur taluk (part of a revenue district). Here lived an equally famous elephant Kandankoran, known for his huge build and the size of his long, curved tusks.

Kandankoran's intelligence was unique. He was good-natured, yet courageous. Periods of *musth* did not affect his nature and he was harmless, even with children who unwittingly strayed close to him. He would not obey any mahout and instead the mahout went along with what the elephant wished. Kandankoran was never tied to a stake. He was free to move as he wished and always found a resting place at night.

He spent most of the day in a river adjoining the temple in the company of a large number of cattle. There were days when these cattle were not fed and on such days Kandankoran would let them into the surrounding sugarcane fields by opening the fence. He would then make mock attacks on anyone who tried to drive the cattle away. However, never once did he cause bodily harm to anyone. Kandankoran would not touch even a stick of sugarcane and would wait for his food provided by the mahout and the temple.

On one night, Kandankoran was resting in the water when a boat carrying spices, arecanut and other commodities came down the river. The boatmen did not see the elephant until the boat had actually hit him. The elephant sank the boat and the boatmen fled for their lives. Thereafter no boat dared pass Kandankoran while he was in the river. The boatmen would stop far away and survey the route ahead. They also began to make offerings to the deity of the temple to ensure their paths did not cross Kandankoran's! With these offerings the temple made a cluster of lamps which exists to this day on its eastern side.

---

*Kitangoor Kandankoran

Kandankoran knew the entire routine to be followed in the temple on ordinary days as well as on special festival days. He knew when to present himself every day to carry the deity around the temple. The person carrying the deity would be helped up by him from the front while all others including those who "dressed" him up with the golden headdress were helped up with his hind leg. On festival days he knew when to walk fast or go slow, where and how long to wait for each stage of the festival. On the late nights of the festival he would be patient. He was so well aware of the correct duration of each ritual that he would not allow any short cuts in this. He would just refuse to move till after the correct time had passed.

There are many stories about Kandankoran's good nature. One of these is narrated here. He was returning from the temple one day when he happened to turn into a very narrow lane and came face to face with an aged Nambudiri woman and her escort. The escort fled and the old woman fell down from sheer fright. Kandankoran stood still for some time, then gently picked up the woman and moved her and her palmyra leaf umbrella to a side before moving on.

Kandankoran was often utilised for moving heavy logs. No log was too heavy or too big for him. However, he would not move a log till he was satisfied that the right compensation had been agreed on and that had to include a share for him. He had six mahouts but he would not move out of the temple without the senior mahout. If Kandankoran was not happy with his reward which was usually bananas, coconuts, and jaggery he would take the log back to its original storage. He was able to understand the terms of the compensation and express approval or otherwise by making sounds or shaking his head. There was an instance of the owner of the logs breaking his promise of compensation for moving some heavy logs. Kandankoran put all the logs back and no other elephant was able to shift them. Kandankoran had to be brought back and the temple authorities and the mahouts were persuaded to agree to the new terms of the compensation. However Kandankoran refused to work and it took much effort before he was convinced enough to resume work.

When The Rulers Spar*

This is a light-hearted narrative of how two local rulers tried to get even with each other.

Once upon a time the Raja of Kolaswarupam went on a visit to the Zamorin. Both of them were rulers who pretended to like each other, observing the courtesies of mutual visits and exchanging compliments. However, they were not really friends with each other.

On this visit, the guest was received by the host with apparent warmth and hospitality and the two were engaged in friendly banter after a lavish meal. In the course of this light-hearted conversation the guest jovially asked his host, "Will the Zamorin sting?" In reply the Zamorin asked his guest, "Will you burn?" The Kolaswarupam ruler said, "Yes, I might burn, be careful," to which the Zamorin replied, "If you could burn then I could sting." This banter ended and it was time for the visitor to depart.

After a long time the Kolaswarupam ruler had a very cleverly designed box made and sent through a messenger to the Zamorin. Apart from the fact that the box was filled with gunpowder, there was also a device to set it off when the box was opened. The box and its key were delivered by the messenger to the Zamorin with an appropriate message. The Zamorin was puzzled by the arrival of this gift and suspected there was something strange about it. He recalled asking the Kolaswarupam ruler whether he would burn and the reply saying he might. He suspected there was something inflammable in the box and that it might explode when the box was opened. He asked his retainers to dip the box in water and bring it back. It was brought back wet and

---

Kolathiriyum Saamoothiriyum
Zamorin – also known as Saamoothiri, ruler of erstwhile Calicut, now called Kozhikode.

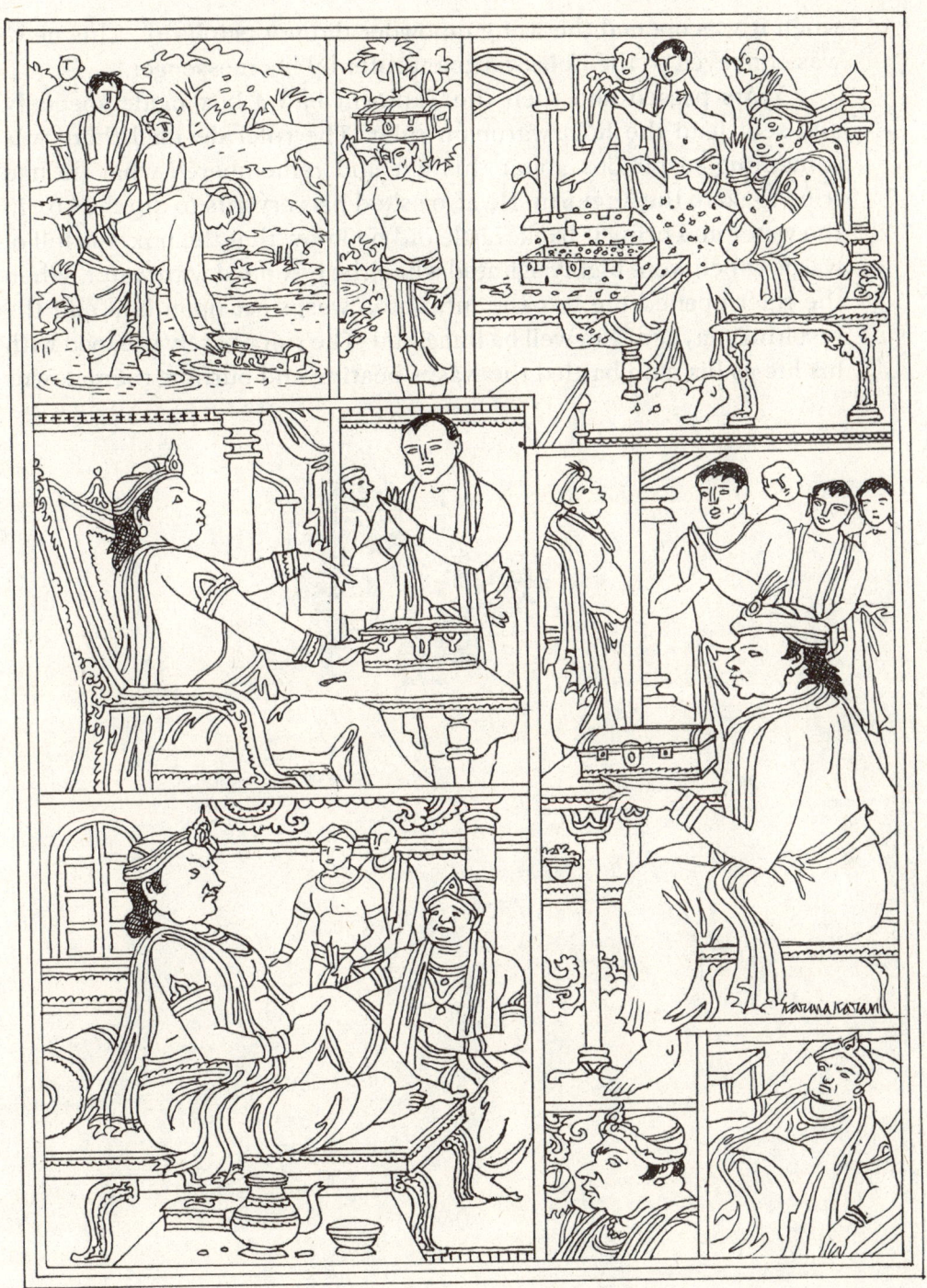

when it was opened the wet gunpowder did not catch fire. This news was conveyed to the Kolaswarupam ruler by his messenger.

Years passed and then the Zamorin had a box made specially and sent it to the Kolaswarupam ruler. The ruler decided there was something suspicious about this gift and remembered what he had tried to do to the Zamorin. He also asked his servants to dip the box in the water and bring it back. Little did he know that the box was full of wasps which were highly agitated when the box filled with water. When the ruler opened the box the infuriated wasps set upon him and the resulting mayhem can well be imagined. The ruler barely escaped with his life as his men battled the wasps beating and burning them down.

Cascade of Genius*

Miracles do take place and hopelessness is replaced by happiness. Here is a story of one such miracle.

The Kottayam‡ principality was at the northern end of British Malabar (which is now part of Kerala State). The members of the Kottayam royal family were all very learned and there was usually not a single unscholarly person amongst them. It so happened just once that a baby was born and grew up displaying no intelligence at all.

As the royalty was still in power and this prince was the eldest male he was given extra academic attention and grooming but to no effect. He was becoming an illustration of the truth that being the son of a scholarly mother, being raised by her and educated by the best teachers available do not necessarily produce the desired result.

The Zamorin (ruler) of Kozhikode (erstwhile Calicut) died and as the two royal families maintained the friendliest of relations, the Kottayam family had to send a male representative on a condolence visit to Kozhikode. The prince's mother agonised over this and finally decided that her son had to go and that precautions had to be taken to prevent a fiasco. She therefore tutored him to repeat three polite enquiries and said that after this the learned members of the royal entourage would take over the conversation. The prince was made to repeat the three words many times each day until his departure. The day finally arrived when the royal party left for Kozhikode where it was received with appropriate honours. The heir to the Kozhikode throne met our hero who made the tutored enquiry, "What can I do for you?" in Sanskrit but got his grammar wrong. The

---

*Kottayathu Raja
‡ There is another Kottayam down south in Central Travancore.

response was a sarcastic one virtually telling him, "You can get your language right." The royal delegation returned in great embarrassment and reported the matter to the queen mother.

The queen mother was in much distress over the unprecedented humiliation to which the family had been subjected. She finally reconciled herself to the futility of having such a son and ordered that he be bound hand and foot and left in Kumaradhara (roughly means a *dhara* or "a cascade of water" falling on a *kumara* or "young man"). This was a waterfall from a ten-man height and the belief was that anyone left under the waterfall would freeze to death or if he or she survived, the person would turn into an intellectual. The prince was dropped under Kumaradhara and when the retainers went to fetch him a day later they found him virtually frozen but still breathing. He was promptly removed to his home where he was attended to with all care.

When the prince recovered fully he was a man transformed. He spoke with great felicity and sweetness of language and the queen mother and others were thrilled at this change. Renowned scholars were engaged as tutors and within a short time he became a scholar in his own right and a poet besides. He also turned out to be a ruler who surpassed his predecessors in administrative skills and fame.

He wrote quite a few verses which became the lyrics for famous dance dramas of Kerala. It was a terrible coincidence that in one of his compositions he had a line which said, "The forest is our only hope," and not long after that the royal family had to seek refuge in the forest when Tipu Sultan marched towards the south.

This ruler was a contemporary of the famed poet and scholar Meppathur Bhattathiri. The family lost their ruling powers long ago but did enjoy some monetary support from the British.

The Tradition of the Magic Herb*

This is the story of one of the eight famous families of renowned Ayurvedic physicians and of divine intervention in their lives.

It was the tradition in the olden days for each of the rulers in Kerala to appoint one of the *Ashtavaidyas* (members of the eight reputed families of Ayurvedic physicians) as his personal physician. The Raja of Cochin appointed Kuttancheri Moos as his physician. An annual remuneration of 152 *puthan*s (a *puthan* was an old silver coin which would be nearly equivalent to the present five paise in numerical but not monetary terms) was paid on the birthday of the ruler.

It is known that raw rice does not suit everyone. The deity of Koodalmanikkam temple in Kerala was apparently one of them. It has been the custom to make an offering of raw rice to this deity every year in the Malayalam month of *Thulam* (roughly October/ November) on *Thiruvonam* day. It was also the tradition that on the following day Brahmins were employed to crush various medicinal herbs for a remedy for stomach disorders which was then offered to the deity. Kuttancheri Moos had the responsibility to supervise the preparation of this offering. He had to arrive at the temple with all the herbs and ingredients on the day before which the raw rice offering was made. Now these herbs and ingredients were known only to the members of Kuttancheri Moos's family. In return for his specialised contribution Moos was given a hundred measures of paddy and one rupee. It was believed that the medicine prepared in the temple could cure all ailments, particularly those to do with the stomach. As a result

Kuttancheri Moos

there were many who thronged the temple on that special day to receive a share of this medicine which was also sent to the Raja of Cochin.

There is a story about how Kuttancheri Moos was invested with the privilege of preparing the medicine every year for the Koodalmanikkam deity. A member of the Kuttancheri family was travelling on foot through Thrissur and by night had reached the paddy fields of Irinjalakuda. The moonlight showed a man sitting by the wayside. As Moos passed him he called out to Moos and asked him who he was, where he was going and such other questions. Then he said, "I am suffering from a bad stomach after a meal of raw rice which is why I am resting here. Please have a remedy prepared by Brahmins and placed outside the sanctum sanctorum of Koodalmanikkam temple. The people there will know what to do thereafter. Even if you do not see me there please assume I am there." Having said this the person vanished.

Kuttancheri Moos was wonderstruck. He was convinced that the person was no ordinary mortal and that he had to be obeyed. He went to the Koodalmanikkam temple and stayed there overnight. Strangely during that same night the functionaries and priests of the temple had a dream in which someone appeared and said, "Tomorrow morning some crushed medicinal herbs will be brought to the sanctum sanctorum. Please have them boiled into a potion and offered to the deity. The person who brings the herbs is to be given a hundred measures of paddy. This offering and the compensation are to be made regularly every year on the day after the offering of raw rice." As each of the functionaries and priests had had the same dream simultaneously, they discussed this phenomenon and decided to consult an astrologer. He confirmed that the person who appeared in the dream was the deity Himself. Meanwhile, Kuttancheri Moos arrived with the crushed herbs and related his experience of the previous night.

The crushed herbs were boiled into a potion and offered to the deity thus commencing a tradition which is followed to this day. So also the compensation of a hundred measures of paddy given annually to Kuttancheri Moos.

The members of Kuttancheri Moos's family who complete their training in medical science do not commence practice till they have spent a year of worship in Nelluvaya temple. The legend behind this is that there were two brothers in the family who were well versed in medicine.

While both of them were equally skilled the elder brother failed to receive as much recognition as the younger one. Those who came for treatment insisted on consulting the younger brother in preference to the elder one.

It so happened that the Zamorin of Kozhikode was ill and the younger Moos was sent for. Unfortunately the younger Moos was on a long journey and the older one offered to go to visit the Zamorin. However, this offer was rejected and the older Moos felt humiliated and depressed. "Oh, my God, why is it that nobody wants me? My brother and I have the same skills but everyone wants him. Why should I live such a life. Maybe I do not have the divine blessing that my brother has and I should seek divine help."

The older brother went to the nearby Nelluvaya temple and worshipped Dhanvanthari, the lord of cures, single-mindedly for a whole year before returning home. His fortunes changed overnight and the demand for his attention grew rapidly. The Zamorin who had only benefited somewhat from the younger brother's treatment sent for the older brother who cured the Zamorin fully over a period of time. The older Moos was well rewarded and from then onwards all the members of the Kuttancheri Moos family have worshipped for a year in Nelluvaya temple before commencing professional practice.

All the members of the Kuttancheri Moos family were trained within the family, never outside. However, they did train students from outside the family. Some of the famed Ashtavaidyas including Eledath Thaikad Moos, Thrissur Thaikad Moos, and Alathur Moos were themselves trained by the Kuttancheri Moos family.

One of the former seniors of the Kuttancheri Moos family was an expert in interpreting the basic document of Ayurvedic medicine, *Ashtangahridaya*. None of the Ashtavaidyas were willing to introduce members of other communities such as Nairs and others to the core meaning of *Ashtangahridaya* but the senior Kuttancheri Moos broke this tradition. He, however, insisted that all those who approached him for training should worship in the local temple during the entire period of their education.

It is also worthy of mention that another senior of the family, a distinguished physician himself, was fortunate enough to forge alliances with most of the other Ashtavaidyas by offering his daughters in marriage to those families!

A Wife's Strategy*

This humorous story illustrates how, with a well crafted message, a wife retrieved her husband from his lover.

It has often been suggested that if wives lack intelligence and stray from the virtuous path it reflects the incompetence of the husbands. It can also be said that when husbands behave the same way the wives are responsible for it. If a husband can motivate his wife to take care of him and be devoted to him, then a wife can manage the husband ten times more easily and ensure that he is totally devoted to her. There are enough examples among our own people of wives and husbands going astray. One such is narrated below.

There was a member of the Idapalli nobility in the old Travancore State who was married in Idapalli but spent all his time in Kallooppara which was a part of his territory where he had a lover. He hardly saw his wife after the marriage rituals were completed. In time the people there began to express their sorrow that even after twelve years of marriage there had been no addition to the family. They anticipated with apprehension the decline of a noted Nambudiri family because of the lack of successors. Nambudiri relations called on the nobleman in Kallooppara and suggested that he should perform appropriate religious ceremonies to become a father or marry again. The hero of our story did not respond favourably but after persistent demands from the others he agreed to re-marry. The Nambudiri relations were under the impression that the wife was incapable of having a child and hence it was that they suggested re-marriage.

The Nambudiri nobleman refused to convey the news to his wife and the other Nambudiris agreed to do that on his behalf. A senior employee of the family went with the Nambudiris to the wife so that the result of the meeting could be conveyed promptly to the husband. The delegation called on the wife and conveyed the proposal to her. She responded thus, "It is necessary that a child is born in the family and I

---

*Oru Antharjanathinte Yukthi

regret it has not happened. I totally agree that my husband should re-marry. However he must take care this time that the horoscope of his future wife is studied carefully so that his first mistake is not repeated. The new horoscope must be different from mine. It must be such that the new wife can have a child in Idapalli even if the husband lives in Kallooppara." The response was duly conveyed to the husband who was overcome by feelings of shame and guilt. He returned to Idapalli without delay and there was no more talk of re-marriage. Not unnaturally a child was born in the family within a year. It was a boy and he was followed by many more.

May our Kerala women display the same tact and the devotion to their husbands as the wife in our story did. May they all thus command the attention of their husbands and live happily.

The Ant-hill Temple*

The is the story of how a powerful Kali temple came to be built under unusual circumstances.

Mandakkat is in South Travancore near the Arabian Sea. There is a Devi temple in this village and this is the story of its origin.

The low caste men of Mandakkat used to take cattle out to graze every day and while at their work, used to play a kind of football using a palm nut. One day while this game was in progress the palm nut happened to hit an ant-hill which cracked. Blood poured from this crack sending all the cowherds into a panic. Some of them fell into a faint and the news soon reached the owners of the cattle and the other residents of the village who rushed to the spot. One of the persons present went into a trance and declared that the ant-hill was in fact the idol of the goddess Kali to be worshipped with prescribed rituals. This would bring prosperity to the area and its people. As for the flow of blood, it could be stopped by applying sandalwood paste to the crack.

Those present summoned an astrologer who confirmed the directions given during the trance. The owner of the land summoned Brahmins who made the sandalwood paste and applied it to the crack, stopping the flow of blood. A thatched shelter was provided for the ant-hill which was also fenced off.

Rituals were performed regularly and large numbers of people visited the temple to worship. Soon it became known that the desires of devotees were fulfilled by prayer at this temple and this attracted even larger crowds. Tuesdays and Fridays were days of special prayer and the offerings of the devotees in cash and kind streamed in. The owner of the land on which the temple stood became a wealthy man.

The idol which was in the shape of the ant-hill grew in size and

---

*Mandakkat Devi

power over time. The owner of the land, however, gradually lost interest in the correct conduct of the rituals and was more interested in acquiring more wealth. At this stage the government paid him off and took over the ownership of the temple. Funds and supervision were provided for the running of the temple and it happened that the idol acquired incredible power striking terror in the hearts of the people who feared to go past the temple even in broad daylight. It was decided that the power of the idol had to be reduced and for this purpose it was decided that rituals would be conducted by lower castes on ordinary days and by Brahmins only on special days. This practice is still sustained.

On Tuesdays hundreds of devotees visit the temple and on the last Tuesday of every month the deity is taken out in a procession in a chariot shaped like the sanctum sanctorum. The crowds were larger on these days and pots of rice were cooked and a large number of the poor were fed.

The annual festival of the temple is held over ten days ending with the last Tuesday of the Malayalam month of *Kumbham* (February/March). Sweets and fruits are offered in large quantities at the temple. The days of the festival are announced months ahead in the government gazette to provide as much notice as possible to the devotees. On these days poultry and animals such as goats were sacrificed to appease the spirits who are part of the deity's following. It is believed that these spirits spread diseases such as small pox and that the sacrifice keep them in good humour, preventing an outbreak and the spread of the disease. The crowds that participated in this festival and the sacrifice were almost entirely from the lower castes. The custom of sacrifice was eventually stopped during the reign of the Maharani Regent of Travancore, Rani Lakshmi Bai.

The government renovated both this temple into a permanent structure to house the idol, and a Shastha temple nearby. During the hot summer the idol does develop cracks but Brahmins are deputed immediately to repair them with sandalwood paste. The old beliefs continue to this day but maybe not as strongly as they used to be.

Neelakantan of Panthalam*

Neelakantan was yet another temple elephant with almost human intelligence and feelings. He was gentle with those who were kind to him but merciless with those who ill-treated him.

Around the Malayalam year 1040 (roughly 1865 in the modern calendar) a group of Arabs was passing through Central Travancore with four elephants. It was dark when they reached the Shiva temple in Panthalam and they were permitted by the temple authorities to tie the elephants to the trees at the eastern entrance of the temple. They then set about cooking their dinner and preparing for the night.

Of the four elephants two were mature ones while the other two were very young. The Arabs and their elephants seemed to know nothing about each other. For instance when they rode on the elephants the Arabs faced the wrong way and they had no idea about managing the elephants. Each of the elephants had a rope round its neck by which it was led by an Arab walking in front. The elephants walking tamely behind the Arabs in their silk robes and wearing their strange headgear was quite a sight!

It was the time of the annual festival in the temple and the local dignitaries had assembled for the occasion. They had found it difficult to hire an elephant to carry the deity in the procession and were, therefore, planning to buy an elephant. As they did not have enough money in the temple coffers they made an offer to the Arabs for the smallest and leanest of the four elephants. They could not agree on the price and the Arabs and their elephants resumed their journey.

They had only covered a short distance when the young elephant for which there was an offer appeared fatigued and stopped in its tracks. No amount of coaxing could persuade it to move and the Arabs decided that taking this weak animal with them would be unwise. They returned

*Panthalam Neelakantan

to the temple and handed over the elephant to the temple for a price lower than was originally offered.

The responsibility of looking after this untrained animal was entrusted to Unnithan who was a renowned trainer of elephants. Unnithan took the elephant for a bath and then presented him in front of the deity. The elephant was named "Neelakantan", one of the names by which Lord Shiva was known. Neelakantan was then fed generously on the offerings of rice, pudding, and other delicious items made regularly to the deity. All these formed Neelakantan's daily menu. He was parked under a make-shift shelter and introduced to the various commands by Unnithan. In six or seven years Neelakantan became a handsome and well-trained elephant.

Unnithan gave way to two full-time mahouts, Madhavashar and his brother Govindashar. Madhavashar looked after Neelakantan with almost paternal love and always addressed him as "My son". Neelakantan received a share of whatever food or drink that Madhavashar had and this included Madhavashar's daily tot of toddy or arrack. On the not infrequent occasions when Madhavashar fell into a drunken stupor Neelakantan would wait patiently by his side till he recovered or even gently carried him home with the trunk. Madhavashar never forced Neelakantan to do hard work or used violence on his animal. When hard work became unavoidable and the wages were good he would encourage Neelakantan with bananas and loving words. Govindashar was exactly the opposite of his brother in his attitude to Neelakantan and his own personal qualities.

One day Govindashar took Neelakantan to the river for a bath. Unnithan also happened to be there which pleased Neelakantan very much. After the bath Neelakantan was standing on the bank of the river when for some reason Govindashar hit Neelakantan. The elephant, not used to such treatment, was enraged and he lashed out at Govindashar with his trunk. Govindashar ducked and Unnithan was felled by the blow. Unnithan managed to rise and flee for his home followed by Govindashar. Neelakantan was sad that he had hit Unnithan and was running aimlessly when Madhavashar appeared. He calmed Neelakantan with loving entreaties. Unnithan did not survive for more than a week.

The news of Unnithan's death caused Neelakantan great sorrow and he refused food and water for three days. It was said that Govindashar plotted Unnithan's death using black magic on Neelakantan. However, it was obvious to all seeing Neelakantan's grief that the elephant would never have deliberately harmed his first teacher.

After Unnithan died Madhavashar became the unquestioned caretaker of Neelakantan and he was understandably happy. So was Govindashar for the different reason that he would be able to secretly use Neelakantan for work for which he could get paid. Soon enough Govindashar did get such an opportunity to have a heavy log moved.

Neelakantan was reluctant to move such a heavy log but tried for fear of being thrashed by the heartless Govindashar. When the log did not move Neelakantan gave up and let go the towing rope. Govindahsar immediately hit him hard and unable to bear the pain Neelakantan tossed Govindashar off his back. As Govindashar fell to the ground Neelakantan stepped on him and Govindashar met a gory end. Neelakantan was in a rage and he ran aimlessly as people fled for shelter. Madhavashar heard about his brother's death and rushed towards Neelakantan despite appeals from his family and friends not to approach an angry Neelakantan. He caught up with Neelakantan, stopped him and gently spoke in his ears. "My son," he said, "How can you do a thing like this? I know he must have ill-treated you but at least in future you should not be so harsh." Neelakantan became calm and followed Madhavashar home.

Madhavashar's affection for Neelakantan was beyond words and this was reflected in Neelakantan's attitude to people whom he never harmed under any circumstances. One day Neelakantan was standing in Madhavashar's yard when he overheard an argument between Madhavashar and his wife. She was complaining that her husband had not brought any firewood for cooking although she had told him to. As the dispute threatened to get out of control Neelakantan walked out, found some driftwood near the river and carried it back bringing the dispute to an end.

There was a plantation in the neighbourhood where the European Manager wished to have a heavy teakwood log shifted. Many elephants tried to shift the log but failed and it was at that point in time that Madhavashar and Neelakantan happened to pass that way. Madhavashar remarked light-heartedly that the job could have been done if there was

one's own elephant, a mahout who loved his animal and an employer who was willing to pay good money for the job. The Manager overheard this and asked Madhavashar how much he would charge for the job. Madhavashar quoted thirty-five rupees and was asked to proceed with the job. Madhavashar went up to Neelakantan and whispered in his ear, "My son, this is a matter of our honour." The log was shifted as required and the Manager not only paid the thirty-five rupees but also fed Neelakantan lavishly with bananas, coconuts, and jaggery. The Manager then asked if Madhavashar would sell his animal. Madhavashar replied, "The elephant belongs to the people of Panthalam and it is unlikely that they will agree to sell Neelakantan. Even if they agreed I will not let them sell Neelakantan for even a hundred thousand rupees."

Elephants have their periods of musth when they are usually not in control of themselves and are hence tethered securely. Neelakantan also had the musth but he was never tethered because he never harmed anybody. There was one occasion when he was in a state of musth and was wandering aimlessly. He came across a group of tribal children seated under a mango tree gorging on the fruits. Seeing Neelakantan the children scattered in all directions but one of them was so overcome with fright that he fainted on the spot holding his mango. Neelakantan picked up this boy gently and deposited him in the tribal hut nearby. The parents were sure their child had been killed by the mad elephant but they soon saw that he was safe and even the mango in his hand had not been disturbed.

On another day Neelakantan strayed into a yard in which was located a little hut where a young, poor woman lived with her toddler daughter. The mother had gone next door to collect water when, seeing Neelakantan, the little girl walked unsteadily towards Neelakantan and hung on to his trunk. The elephant managed to extricate himself from the girl's embrace, lifted the little girl and placed her back in the hut.

Neelakantan was once walking through a lane in his musth state when one of the workers picked up a stone and threw it at the elephant's head and fled. The elephant went after him, broke through a wall and entered a yard. The occupants were terrified and pleaded with him not to harm them. Neelakantan pursued the person who pelted him, caught up with him, and felled him with the same stone.

Thus Neelakantan became a handsome animal over the years and was in great demand for temple processions in the area. He understood the rituals and knew the nature and time of his task in each temple which he fulfilled without any prompting.

Madhavashar died of small pox leaving Neelakantan distraught. It took seven days for Neelakantan to regain his calm and resume eating. Thereafter Neelakantan had a string of mahouts who did not love him and on the other hand ill-treated him. They lasted but a few months each before they fell victim to the elephant's rage.

It was in 1080 Malayalam Era (1905 by the modern calendar) that Neelakantan died while working in a plantation. The cause of his death is presently unknown and there has been much speculation about it. All that matters now is that Neelakantan was unique in his behavioural instincts and physical features. Some of the reports of his intelligence and affection may appear to be exaggerated but at the time of writing there are still many who have seen Neelakantan and confirm the truth of these reports.

A Fiery Penance*

A favoured disciple condemns himself to a fiery death for harbouring thoughts of violence against his guru who drove him harshly towards excellence.

There are few who have not heard of the eminent poet Prabhakaran who wrote those famous verses of *Krishna Vilasam*. He was also known as Sukumaran and was a Brahmin.

Prabhakaran was a bright, attentive and devoted disciple and a favourite of his guru. However, the guru treated him harshly all the time, scolding and slapping him more than he did the other disciples who were less intelligent. He would repeat a meaning or an explanation many times for the other students whereas he insisted that Prabhakaran should arrive at the meaning or find an explanation himself. If the guru had to help he would do it just once. Prabhakaran was quick to grasp complicated matters in his studies but he was always criticized by his guru as a dunce and a laggard. His conversation with Prabhakaran was only in angry tones. Prabhakaran pursued his studies with total devotion enduring the harsh treatment with great patience and without any resentment. He eventually became well versed in poetry, drama and the scriptures but neither he nor his teacher considered it necessary to terminate his studies.

Prabhakaran grew into a learned and handsome youth studying new and increasingly difficult subjects. The treatment meted out by the guru continued to be the same. One day Prabhakaran asked his guru for help in understanding a part of his lesson. The guru flew into a rage, abused Prabhakaran for being a fool and started thrashing him mercilessly. Prabhakaran"s thigh started bleeding and unable to bear the pain, he fled and hid himself. The thrashing affected Prabhakaran deeply, his resentment over the unfair treatment grew and he decided to take revenge against his teacher. When the teacher had gone for his evening ablutions Prabhakaran found a boulder which he hefted into

---

*Prabhakaran

the attic above the teacher's bedroom with the intention of dropping it on the teacher to kill him.

The teacher returned home but refused to have his dinner pleading illness. He went to his bedroom and lay down on his bed. His wife also did not eat and followed her husband into the bedroom to find out the nature of his illness. The guru explained, "There is nothing much wrong with me except that I thrashed Prabhakaran far too much in anger. I feel very sad that I did and Prabhakaran who usually endures all this patiently ran away today. He just could not bear the pain and as for me my heart bleeds for Prabhakaran. I just could not bear to eat dinner." His wife said to him, "It is really sad and I have been wishing to talk to you about this but did not fearing you may not like it. I cannot think of anybody as bright, good-natured, and devoted as Prabhakaran but you abuse and thrash him. How can you treat someone who is mentally and physically so perfect as cruelly as you do? He is no longer a child and it is not right that you should treat a youth as if he were a child – and he is not even our child."

The guru agreed with his wife and confessed, "I have never considered Prabhakaran as another's child. In fact I love him more than I love my own son. I know his qualities of head and heart and love him very much indeed. I did not wish to display my love and admiration for him lest he be filled with arrogance and lose interest in his studies. The result of my harsh treatment will be seen later when Prabhakaran becomes the greatest scholar in the world. I admit I went beyond limits today and I am deeply distressed. I shall never again hurt him in any way."

Prabhakaran listened to the entire conversation and his anger against his teacher disappeared altogether and his respect and regard grew enormously. He was filled with remorse for having made diabolic plans against his guru. He descended from his perch in the attic and fell at the *guru*'s feet. The guru was overcome by emotion as he raised Prabhakaran from the ground and embraced him warmly. Neither could speak for a while. The guru then apologized profusely for his past behaviour and swore never to hurt Prabhakaran again.

Prabhakaran then made his confession to his teacher. "You may scold and beat me as much as you like and I shall take both happily. Unable to bear the pain of your last thrashing some evil thoughts entered my mind. I planned to kill you which was why I was hiding in the attic. Please forgive me and advise me what I have to do to cleanse myself of the sin I have committed."

The guru assured him that remorse was the ultimate penance and that he had been forgiven. Prabhakaran, however, was not satisfied and insisted on harsher punishment. The guru then suggested that Prabhakaran should consult the council of Brahmins on the matter which Prabhakaran did. The council pronounced that the penalty for wishing to kill one's teacher was death in a burning heap of paddy husks.

Prabhakaran accordingly arranged for paddy husks to be heaped up to his neck and ignited. In order to be remembered after his death he commenced dictating the now famous verses of *Krishna Vilasam* as the fire slowly consumed him. The verses ended abruptly at the twelfth canto as the fire reached his throat.

In later years the renowned Kalidasa decided to complete the verses but the legend is that a divine voice ordered him not to join "a silken thread to a fibre from the banana tree." *Krishna Vilasam* was left incomplete.

The Power of Mime*

The power of mime as practised in Kathakali, the famous dance drama of Kerala, is illustrated in this narration.

In Kathakali, the dance drama of Kerala, Ammannur Parameswara Chakyar was unsurpassed in his costume sense and miming talent. His residence was in a village called Muzhikkulam but he nearly always travelled at the invitation of rulers and other dignitaries of Cochin, Travancore, and British Malabar (now forming the composite Kerala State).

In the middle of the eighteenth century, *Elaya Raja* Marthanda Varma of Travancore enlisted Parameswara Chakyar's service to train one of his staff in Kathakali. His training was so effective that his student became known for his ability to use mime to describe heaven, the ocean, and such other subjects.

On one of his visits to Marthanda Varma's palace he was invited to watch a Kathakali performance. The scene was of the demon king Ravana lifting the Kailasa mountain and at the end of the performance Marthanda Varma asked Chakyar for his assessment of the show. Chakyar's cautious reply was, "Not bad but I thought Kailasa was much bigger," which was a reference to the mime. Marthanda Varma then expressed a desire to see Chakyar's version of the same scene. He was reluctant to perform without the appropriate costume and make-up but he obliged, clad in whatever he was wearing then. All those who had participated in the earlier performance and Marthanda Varma's wife were there to watch as Chakyar commenced his version. Needless to say he excelled himself and so impressive was he that Marthanda Varma's wife exclaimed, "I did not know Kailasa was so big," which was a compliment to Chakyar's genius for mime.

On another occasion, Chakyar was in Trivandrum (now Thiruvananthapuram) and decided to stroll along the seashore. There

---

*Ammannur Parameswara Chakyar

were many locals and Europeans also enjoying their evening walk. Among them were the British Resident (local representative of the British Crown) and his wife with their fierce-looking dog. This dog was harmless but it had a habit of smelling all those around its owners. The dog approached Chakyar who was frightened by the dog and started shouting, "Dog! Dog!" Knowing that the dog was harmless the Resident and his wife did not call the dog back and instead burst out laughing at Chakyar's predicament. Chakyar resorted to his only means of self-defence – mime. He pretended to bend down, pick up a stone and fling it at the dog. So realistic was his action that the dog fled yelping as if it had indeed been struck by the stone. The Resident and his wife believed that the dog had been hit and were enraged. On enquiry, they found that the culprit, Chakyar, was a guest of Marthanda Varma and decided to complain directly to him. Chakyar was sent for and he explained all that had happened. The Resident and his wife were emphatic in their belief that their dog had been hit and that the dog could not be fooled by mere pretence. In order to lay this matter to rest Marthanda Varma asked Chakyar whether he could prove the power of mime for the benefit of the foreigners.

There was a huge granite step leading up to the palace and Chakyar went through the motions of lifting it with great difficulty. Having done that, Chakyar pretended to throw it at the Resident's head. The Resident screamed as if in pain and fell into a faint. His wife was struck dumb. It was some time before the Resident recovered and felt his head to check for any injury. He was finally convinced that the granite step was not thrown at him in which case, he realized, the dog also may not have been hit.

The Resident and his wife were so taken up by the impressive performance of Chakyar that they rewarded him with many gifts. They apologized profusely for their behaviour and left for their residence where their dog had also returned unharmed. All was well in the end!

God vs. God*

One sees human beings disagreeing with each other but hardly expects their gods to engage in petty competition.

During Tipu Sultan's conquest of the south the deity of the famous Guruvayur temple near Thrissur in the erstwhile Cochin State was removed first to Aranmula and then to Mavelikkara, both in the former Travancore State. Although the Guruvayur and Aranmula deities are different forms of the same Lord Krishna, legend has it that during this period they did display their disapproval of each other.

In Guruvayur the offering of *kaalan*, a curry of yoghurt and yam, made to the Guruvayur deity would keep for days without turning sour or becoming inedible. However, while the deity was in Aranmula it was noticed that the same curry turned inedible within a short time. It was the belief that the Aranmula deity was responsible for this.

The main offering in the Aranmula temple is a delicious milk and rice pudding. During the Guruvayur deity's stay in Aranmula it was seen that when the pudding was offered to the deity various impurities surfaced making this ritual impossible. One does not have to guess who the guilty party was in this case!

The Vaikom and Ettumanur deities also have been known to show displeasure against each other. Back in the Malayalam year 973 (corresponding to 1798 in the modern calendar) the Maharaja of Travancore had eight elephants made of wood and plated in gold and sent them as his offering to the Vaikom temple. These were being carried under escort by road and after a day's journey they reached the Ettumanur temple. The elephants were handed over for safekeeping to the local guards while the Maharaja's men went to bathe and eat. When they returned to recover the elephants they found that every single elephant had a serpent seated on it, hood spread menacingly. Unable to approach the elephants the Maharaja's men reported this to the ruler who consulted

*Chila Eashwaranmaarute Pinakkam

astrologers to know the cause of this strange development. The finding was that the Ettumanur deity was unwilling to let go of the elephants which He claimed for Himself. The Maharaja had a dream the same night confirming this finding. These elephants were surrendered to the Ettumanur deity and are even now on display in the annual festival in the temple.

The Maharaja decided to have another eight elephants made for the Vaikom deity as was originally intended when he had a dream. In this dream the Vaikom deity informed the ruler that He did not wish to have the elephants but instead he preferred a special ritual at the same cost. This was done and it is believed that the two deities are not on good terms even to this day. While one cannot confirm this it is the practice for the Ettumanur residents to boycott the Vaikom celebrations on a particular Ashtami day every year.

Two other deities who are known to be not "on speaking terms" with each other are Aranmula Krishnan and Shabarimala Ayyappan. It is said that many years ago some of the Aranmula residents entered into the period of fasting preparatory to a pilgrimage to Shabarimala. The Aranmula deity appeared in a dream advising them against going on this pilgrimage. The pilgrims disregarded the advice and the only concession they made was that they replaced the traditional cries of "Sharanam Ayyappa" invoking the protection of the Shabarimala deity with "Aranmula Swamiye Sharanam" seeking the Aranmula deity's protection. As the pilgrims were walking through the forest they saw their path blocked by tigers.

Stricken with terror they shouted even more loudly to the Aranmula deity. Suddenly a rain of arrows fell on the tigers which fled into the forest. It was obvious that the arrows were sent by the Aranmula deity. At that time Shabarimala Ayyappan decreed through a medium that Aranmula residents were not to set foot in His temple. The pilgrims were forced to return home and there were no further pilgrims for Shabarimala from Aranmula.

There are many more such legends about gods in rivalry with each other. It is not illogical to think that these could have originated from fertile human minds.

A Kerala-style Robin Hood*

The exploits of the Kerala version of Robin Hood, seen by many to be a heartless dacoit but who was actually honest and compassionate.

There cannot be anyone – not just in Travancore – anywhere in Kerala who has not heard of Kayamkulam Kochunni. He appears to have been known as a robber and a criminal whereas in actual fact he was an honest and decent man.

Kochunni was born in the year 993 of the Malayalam Era (corresponding to 1818 in the Gregorian calendar) in Karthikapalli taluk of Travancore State. His father was a known criminal who lived off the proceeds of his thefts. This meant that if his father did not go thieving one night his family starved the next day.

It was with great difficulty that Kochunni lived with his family till the age of ten after which he left home, unable to bear the pangs of hunger. He went to the neighbouring Evoor where he approached a Brahmin family located beside a temple and introduced himself as a Muslim boy who had left home out of sheer poverty. The head of the family took pity on the poor boy and gave him a meal of rice gruel which to Kochunni tasted like nectar!

Kochunni was asked if he would be willing to stay in that area if he were assured of food. Kochunni readily agreed and the Brahmin recommended him to a well-known grocer who gave him a job as a helper. The shopkeeper was so happy with Kochunni's work that he provided Kochunni with food and clothes. Over a few years Kochunni was entrusted with more onerous work such as weighing and measuring out provisions for sale. Eventually he earned the full trust of his employer.

---

*Kayamkulam Kochunni

It so happened that the shopkeeper had to go to Alapuzha to make wholesale purchases and he took Kochunni with him. As they were returning by boat a violent squall lashed the backwaters raising huge waves and threatening to overturn the boat. The boatman cried out helplessly and very soon the shopkeeper and he planned to abandon the boat and the cargo. At this stage Kochunni took over the boat and assured the others that God would save them. He then managed to pole the boat to its destination and safety. Very pleased with Kochunni's pluck and ability his employer decided to pay him not merely his expenses but also a sum over and beyond that. Kochunni did not keep any money for himself but promptly passed it on to his parents.

Kochunni soon got to know that a *Thangal* or a Muslim expert in martial arts was training young Muslims. Kochunni went to the expert one evening after work and asked to join his class. The Thangal refused to enrol him saying that Kochunni's father was a known criminal and with training in martial arts Kochunni would become an even worse criminal. Dejected as he was at this rejection Kochunni did not give up trying to learn martial skills. After work every night he would head for the venue of the training and watch every move from a vantage point, unknown to and unseen by the expert. Thus he came to acquire great expertise in the martial arts until one day he was noticed and his ploy reported to the Thangal. Kochunni was promptly summoned by the Thangal and asked about the extent of the knowledge he had gained. Kochunni honestly answered that he had learnt whatever was taught in the training sessions. The Thangal tested his skills and was pleasantly surprised to see that he had indeed mastered the martial skills. Kochunni was permitted thereafter to attend the class regularly and was taught acrobatic feats as well as special skills of disguise, hypnotism and so on. He then paid the fees, asked for the Thangal's blessings and took his leave. Back at work he was helped by his employer to learn to read and write the local regional languages Tamil and Malayalam.

In course of time the employer came to know that Kochunni had acquired great skills in the martial arts as well as in acrobatics, disguise etc. He decided to part company with Kochunni but on very friendly terms and with mutual assurances of assistance when needed.

Kochunni soon lost his parents but married and brought his wife home. With no resources of any kind he was soon compelled to form a gang and resort to criminal acts such as smuggling, burglary, and highway robbery. He never harmed the poor and the honest but focussed on cruel, rich, and tight-fisted people. His style was to approach such rich people and ask for money. If the money was given he would leave quietly but if it was refused he would take it by some means or the other. Money willingly given was often returned with interest. The extorted money was shared between him and his followers, and from his own share he gave a part to the needy regardless of caste or creed.

Kochunni was involved with loose women and many in the profession flourished thanks to his patronage. One of them in particular was treated by him as his second wife. By this time Kochunni had achieved great notoriety and the Government was eager to capture him. In 1025 Malayalam Era (or 1850 according to the calendar in usage now) the Dewan of the State issued instructions to the *tahsildar* of the Karthikapalli taluk that Kochunni was to be captured within a week. Through his secret sources the *Tashildar* knew that Kochunni had a local woman whom he visited regularly and that this woman had another lover who was no friend of Kochunni's. Through this lover the woman was contacted and bribed with offers of money and position to drug Kochunni's milk that night to render him unconscious. The woman acted accordingly, the unconscious Kochunni was taken captive and carried bound hand and foot by the waiting policemen to the local cell. The Tahsildar was informed who in turn passed on the news to the *Dewan* who ordered that Kochunni should be sent to Thiruvananthapuram under secure escort.

On the morning after Kochunni was taken prisoner he regained consciousness and realized that he had been betrayed by his lover. He waited till late into the night when he managed to break out of the cell and flee. He decided to go to his lover's house and recover his weapon.

He went there and found the door ajar and the woman and her other lover engaged in light-hearted conversation. His entry stunned them and as they cowered behind a screen, Kochunni pulled out his weapon from under the bed. In a single stroke he beheaded both the betrayers. He then left for his own home where his wife was in agony over his reported arrest. She had not eaten since the news reached her. It was with difficulty that he persuaded his wife to open the door but then she hastily cooked some food which both ate heartily. Thereafter Kochunni swore never again to abandon his wife, a promise he kept till the end of his days.

Kochunni's escape created a sensation and gave rise to many rumours about how he could have broken out of the cell. The authorities knew that it was Kochunni who had murdered the woman and her lover and policemen were deployed to recapture him. Kochunni managed to elude the police and soon reports began to reach the government of his renewed criminal activity. He waylaid rich people who travelled along the roads and when the police tried to arrest him on land they would hear that he and his followers had extorted money from those who journeyed by boat. Meanwhile Kochunni's family had increased by three sons and a daughter.

Eighteen years passed with Kochunni eluding the authorities and then his fortunes seemed to change. Sir T. Madhavarayar became Dewan and he was an able administrator who planned to introduce far-reaching reforms in the State. Among his plans was the one to capture Kochunni and free the public from his harassment. For this purpose he brought in Kunju Panikkar as the Tahsildar of Karthikapalli with special instructions to capture Kochunni. Panikkar knew he could not succeed without the assistance of someone close to Kochunni. He managed by means of bribes to enlist the help of a man named Mohammed who was once close to Kochunni but was discarded when he began to torment the poor. Through Mohammed some other followers of Kochunni were also persuaded to secretly change sides.

One night, one of Kochunni's closest friends, Kochupilla, invited Kochunni home and plied him with drugged drinks. Kochunni lost consciousness and his turncoat followers and others tied him to the cot. Kochunni opened his eyes in a drugged haze and saw some of his followers around him. He warned them that they would meet the same fate as his former lover. Kochunni was removed to the police station securely bound to the cot. In the police station he was heavily manacled and sent under armed escort to Thiruvananthapuram. He was taken to

A Kerala-style Robin Hood

the Dewan's presence and then to police custody. Steps were taken to put him on trial with the least delay. The followers of Kochunni who betrayed him were amply rewarded with official positions but very soon they all were involved in offences of various kinds and put into the same jail as Kochunni. After ninety-one days in jail Kochunni died in his forty-first year.

We have till now dwelt upon Kayamkulam Kochunni's criminal activities and made only a passing reference to his kind-heartedness and honesty. It would be unjust to Kochunni if we did not give at least a couple of instances of these qualities.

There was a Brahmin who had to go to his uncle's house in Evoor to deliver jewellery worth five hundred rupees and some cash in preparation for a wedding. This had to be handed over that night and his route took him through Kochunni's territory. He was terrified that he might come face to face with Kochunni and lose his precious belongings but at the same time he had no option but to take that risk. He hoped that he would be able to find another person on the way to keep him company. He set out with his cloth bundle securely tied. When he had travelled some distance and dusk was setting in he saw a man standing on the road. He decided to ignore the man and walk hurriedly past him. The man, however, called out to him, "Ei! Where are you going? Let me talk to you." "I am going to Evoor," the Brahmin replied, "I am in a hurry and have no time to wait and talk to you." The man cautioned him, "I suggest you spend the night somewhere and go tomorrow. Have you heard of Kayamkulam Kochunni? What have you got in your bundle? It looks heavy." The Brahmin would not be dissuaded from continuing his journey. He said, "I cannot stay here tonight as I have to reach Evoor. If you know someone here who would escort me I shall pay him something reasonable." Further negotiations followed in the course of which the Brahmin revealed that his uncle lived near the temple in Evoor and that an escort to Evoor would be paid three rupees. The man said the uncle and he were known to each other and that he would himself escort the Brahmin to Evoor.

By this time night had fallen and it was pitch dark when they commenced their journey to Evoor. On the way the Brahmin expressed his disapproval of persons like Kayamkulam Kochunni and their harassment of travellers. They finally reached the eastern side of the Evoor temple at which point the escort asked to be paid off. The Brahmin thanked his escort and asked him into his uncle's house so that the money could be taken out of the bundle. However his companion chose to wait outside.

The uncle was relieved to see his nephew reach safely and proceeded to pay off the escort while the nephew had a bath and his dinner. He went out of the house and was taken aback when the escort approached him and prostrated before him. The uncle looked at the escort in the light of the lamp and asked, "Oh, aren't you Kochunni? For the help you have given you should be paid not just three rupees but much more. How much would you like?" Kochunni replied with great humility, "I don't want anything at all. I can never forget your act of kindness when I came to you years ago and you fed me and got me employed. I quoted a price merely to test whether your nephew was a man of his word and find out if he was indeed your nephew. All I wish to have is your blessing." He then took leave of the uncle with folded hands and departed.

There is also the story of the Syrian Christian in Kochunni's neighbourhood who lived by selling copra or dried coconut. He used to buy coconut on credit, dry the coconut, and then sell the copra for a meagre profit. He paid for the coconuts promptly after selling the copra and was, therefore, considered very trustworthy. One day he was returning from Alapuzha after selling a large quantity of copra for which he had hired a boat. He had paid for the boat and was going home with two hundred rupees folded in his *dhoti*. He was nervous about travelling at that time of night but he had no alternative. He was halfway to his house when he suddenly found his path blocked by someone. It was when he came close that he recognized Kochunni and was overcome by fright. Kochunni questioned him on his business, reason for his journey that night and how much money he carried. The poor man answered Kochunni truthfully. Kochunni asked him to hand over the money or face the consequences. The poor man handed over the money and Kochunni disappeared with it.

The poor Christian returned home in despair and narrated his experience to his wife. She was happy Kochunni had not taken her

A Kerala-style Robin Hood

husband's life. They were in agony over their inability to pay those from whom he had bought the coconut and wondered how they could get coconuts on credit in the future. Finally they decided they would raise money by mortgaging their little house and thus repay the debt. They could neither eat nor sleep but dawn came and they mortgaged the house and raised some money. The copra business continued as before.

At dusk a few days later, the poor Christian was seated on his verandah when he saw someone approaching him. When the person came close the Christian saw it was Kochunni and jumped up terrified. Kochunni calmed him down and said, "Please don't be afraid. I have come to return the money I took from you the other night. I did not intend to take your money but I was desperately in need myself and I was forced to do what I did. I have some money now and I am returning yours. You may find a bit more than I had taken but that is for your kindness and help." Kochunni handed over a bag and left. The poor man opened the bag and could not believe his eyes when he counted not two hundred rupees but five hundred. Needless to say his business prospered thanks to Kochunni's honesty and generosity.

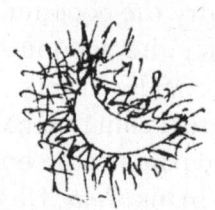

Fate changed by Faith*

*A person fated to die on a certain day was given
an extra lease of life because of his resolve to put his
noble thoughts into practice.*

There was a wealthy Nambudiri in British Malabar whose horoscope
said that at the age of thirty-two he would face serious problems and
die. When he completed thirty-two years he was naturally depressed but
tried to console himself with the thought that not all horoscopes were
fully correct. However, he decided to take his horoscope to the most
eminent of all astrologers, Pazhur Kaniyar. He reached Kaniyar's house
in the evening and explained his predicament. Kaniyar could tell from
merely looking at the Nambudiri that his days were numbered and that
in fact he could fall dead any moment. So he told the Nambudiri that
it was too late that day and it would be better if he rested somewhere
that night and returned the next morning.

The Nambudiri bathed in the river nearby and went to the Pazhur
temple to worship Lord Shiva. While in the temple he was caught in
a thunderstorm and the temple offered him no shelter as it was in a
dilapidated state. The state of the temple saddened the Nambudiri and
it was weighing heavily on his mind as he went to a nearby Nambudiri
house to spend the night. He could not sleep as he was deeply affected
by the broken down temple building. He decided to renovate the temple
and as soon as dawn broke he went to the river for a bath and made
his way again to the temple. He prayed to Lord Shiva and then headed
for Kaniyar's residence.

Kaniyar was surprised to see the Nambudiri alive as he was certain
that the Nambudiri would have died the previous night. He said to the
Nambudiri, "You must have done something very noble last night, what
was it?" The Nambudiri replied that he could think of no such noble
deed. All he had done was to visit the temple and rest that night. Kaniyar
was persistent that the Nambudiri had indeed done something out of the

---

Pazhur Perumthrikkovil

ordinary. If he had not done anything then he must have entertained some noble thoughts. The Nambudiri then explained how sad he was to see the Shiva temple in a state of utter disrepair and how he planned to renovate the temple. Kaniyar then realized that the Nambudiri's fate had been changed by his resolve to build the temple anew. He told the Nambudiri that his worship of Shiva in the temple and his decision to rebuild the temple had saved him. The work was to start without delay and he would live to be a hundred.

The Nambudiri returned home and made arrangements to reconstruct the temple. This he did on the lines of the famous Vaikom temple. He lived on for many years thereafter and died after he had reached a hundred years of age.

The Power of Simplicity*

*How a simple man who sinned in ignorance
went on a pilgrimage where his faith and belief helped him attain
moksha or salvation.*

The Azhuvancheri family of Nambudiris had a large number of cattle and these were looked after by a neighbour, Mangalath Sankaran, a simple man whose only income was from this occupation. He would take the cattle out to graze in the morning and bring them back home late in the evening. With about hundred to hundred and fifty animals and only Sankaran to manage them the task was not easy at all. The cattle would disappear in different directions and would not heed his calls to come back. Out of sheer despair one day he took his stick and beat one of the disobedient animals which promptly fell down and died. Sankaran made a note of where on the body of the cow the blow fell and thereafter every animal which strayed away received a blow in the same place. Needless to say, the animal died and over time the number of cattle dwindled.

One day the head of the Nambudiri family decided to take a look at his cattle. He was shocked to find that the stalls were mostly empty and the few cattle that were there seemed starved. He summoned Sankaran and asked him what had happened to the large herd which was originally there. The simple man that Sankaran was, he spoke with indignation about the recalcitrant animals and how these had been dealt with in the interests of discipline. The Nambudiri was shocked to hear the story and cried out in despair fearing divine retribution for the slaughter of the animals considered sacred. Sankaran was equally desperate when the Nambudiri explained to him the seriousness of his crime. He was eager to atone for his sin and the Nambudiri advised him that a pilgrimage to Kashi (Benares) and a bath in the holy Ganges were the only course open to him.

---

*Mangalath Sankaran

Sankaran bid the Nambudiri farewell and left for Benares. Meanwhile in Benares, the deity of the temple, Vishwanatha or Shiva, was asked by his consort, Parvathi, whether all the thousands who visited Kashi for a bath in the holy Ganges would receive moksha or salvation. Lord Shiva replied that only the ones who had faith and belief in what they did would attain moksha and a mere dip in the holy Ganges would not serve any purpose. He promised Parvathi he would illustrate this the next day.

Sankaran reached Kashi at this time and he went to the banks of the Ganges for his bath. Lord Shiva was also there in the form of an aged Brahmin, with Parvathi posing as his wife. The old man entered the water, slipped and fell into the river where he began to struggle. His wife immediately began to scream for help saying her husband could not swim. A number of people including Sankaran rushed towards the Brahmin when the wife shouted, "Only those cleansed of their sins should touch my husband as otherwise he will die." Most of the people stopped, wondering whether they were really cleansed of their sins and not wishing to be the cause of a Brahmin's death. Sankaran, on the other hand, believed that his bath in Ganges had cleansed him and so he waded into the water and pulled the Brahmin to safety. As the couple was leaving Shiva told Parvathi, "The only one who will attain moksha from among all those who bathed in Ganges is the man who pulled me out. He was the only one who had faith in his bath and himself." Having completed his pilgrimage and worshipped Kashi Vishwanatha, Sankaran stayed on in Kashi till the end of his days.

The Nambudiri family, in the meantime, was beginning to decline in numbers with a fall in new births in the family. Astrologers were summoned to ascertain the cause of this problem which was eventually traced back to the slaughter of the cows. In atonement, the family was advised to grow lentils on a large tract of land and provide free access to cattle to feed on the crops. This was done without delay and soon many children were born in the *illam*.

The head of the family took two major decisions which are respected to this day. One was never to keep cattle and the other was to continue to grow lentils and feed them to cattle from outside.

The Power of Simplicity

The Dilemma of Bigamy*

*How the youthful prank of friends led a not-so-bright youth
to nights of revelry with a divine spirit, with
unexpected consequences.*

In the Venmani family which lived in Vellarapilly in the erstwhile
Cochin State, was a boy who was intellectually backward. His father
did all that was needed to be done in his boyhood and then sent him
to the Brahmin lodge in Thrissur where young Nambudiris lived and
learnt the scriptures. He was treated with contempt by his lodge mates,
teased and bullied.

It was at that time that an artist painted the picture of a divine
spirit on the wall of the sanctum sanctorum of the famous Shiva temple
in Thrissur. The picture was so complete in every respect that the spirit
came to life and took up residence in the picture. She left the temple
at night and roamed around looking for young men to sleep with. Many
young men were harassed by her. There were others who were unable
to fulfil her needs and died in the attempt. A few were left weak and
unable to move. As nobody knew where she would strike next, the men
in that town lived in fear. It became known that if anyone went near the
picture and invited her to spend the night with him she would oblige.

One evening the young men living in the Brahmin lodge went to
the temple to worship there and among them was the young Venmani
Nambudiri. They worshipped the various deities there and when they
were near the picture they persuaded Venmani to invite the spirit to
spend the night with him. He repeated what his friends had told him
to say without knowing the consequences. They returned to the lodge,
finished their evening ablutions, had dinner, and retired for the night.
In the dead of the night the spirit arrived and gently touched Venmani
who woke up immediately. They had an exciting night together and
Venmani who had led a celibate life till then was introduced to the
ultimate pleasures of feminine company. Close to dawn the spirit

---

*Venmani Namburippadanmar

took her leave but Venmani asked her if she would visit him again the following night. She replied, "If you are happy with me and satisfied I shall see you again, not just tonight but every night. However, there is a condition. You are not to touch another woman without my permission for if you do you will never see me again." Venmani promised to abide by the condition. The spirit visited Venmani every night and after a while they fell in love with each other.

The time soon came for Venmani to terminate his studies in Thrissur and return home. His father arrived to take him back home and Venmani was very unhappy over the prospect of his having to give up his divine lover. That night he broke the news to her and asked her what he should do. She reassured him and said he could go with his father. She would continue to visit him every night. They then spent that night as usual revelling in each other's company.

Very soon the father decided that his son should get married and collected a few horoscopes of potential brides. Venmani was again in a dilemma and not in a mood to give up his divine companion. He conveyed to his father his reluctance to get married and the father was enraged. He spoke to his son most harshly, "You will not get married, will you? You are such a fool. Here I am waiting to see my grandchildren before I close my eyes. Do you know this family needs to be sustained and for that you have to get married and have children?" The son continued to reject the idea of marriage and was not willing to give his reason. In despair the father refused to have anything more to do with his son whom he ordered out of his sight.

Venmani was so distraught over his disagreement with his father that he went to bed without eating his dinner. When the spirit arrived for the night she found him crying in bed. She tried to ascertain the reason for his plight but he was reluctant to answer. After much persuasion he revealed the truth. His lover was again very reassuring and asked him to go ahead with the marriage as, if he did not, it would put the future of the family at risk. Her only request was that he should not abandon her. He could sleep with his wife and lover on alternate nights for which he had to make the necessary arrangements. They then spent the night in great happiness.

Venmani went to see his father the next morning and informed him that the marriage plans could proceed as intended. The marriage was conducted in style and Venmani entered his new life as agreed with his lover. He slept with his wife one night and with his lover in another bed the next. Time passed and the wife became pregnant. A son was soon born and he was brought up according to tradition with all rituals being performed on time as desired by the grandfather. The grandfather soon died after realizing his ambition to see his grandchild.

The boy reached the age when the sacred thread ceremony had to be performed. Arrangements were made for this on a large scale and a number of guests were invited. On the eve of the ceremony it was the lover's turn and she was informed of the ceremony to be conducted the next morning. The spirit then said, "I have a wish. Although your wife has married you according to tradition I am really your first wife and your son's aunt. As part of tomorrow's ritual your son has to collect alms and it is my desire that I should be the first to give him alms. I shall come tomorrow for the ceremony disguised as a Nambudiri lady." Venmani assured her that her wish would be fulfilled and that she could attend the ceremony.

By dawn the next day all the guests and families were bathed and dressed as required by custom. The ceremony commenced and soon a Nambudiri lady was seen arriving hidden behind the traditional palm thatch umbrella. Venmani recognized her immediately but whispers went round among the other guests questioning the identity of the strange guest. When the hour came for the ritual collection of alms Venmani instructed the priest to take the boy to the new guest first. The priest refused saying it was against rules which required that the mother should start the ritual. Venmani said the guest was the boy's aunt as he had married her first. This revelation caused an uproar. Those present demanded to know how Venmani could have married without their knowing about it and where the lady was from.

As for the mother she was incensed when she knew that another lady was to start the ritual. She abused the guest and threatened to beat her up if she insisted on giving alms first. Venmani stood silent and alone, unable to say anything. The spirit stood firm and said she had been permitted by the father to lead the ritual. She would do exactly as she had planned. The mother was in a towering rage by now and mobilised her friends and relations to throw the guest out bodily. They pushed and pulled the guest out of the house and onto the street while Venmani ran after them crying out helplessly.

The spirit assumed her real form on the street and addressed Venmani, "You do not have to feel guilty or sad as I do not hold you responsible for my humiliation. However, there will be no occasion for a similar ceremony for a boy in this family beyond three generations from now. Two men in the second generation from now will be acclaimed scholars by the blessing of goddess Saraswathi. As for me I shall not be accepted back in my world after my relationship with the mortal world and in any case I do not wish to live after the humiliation I have been through. You must now go back to complete the ceremony and live happily with your family. You must not grieve for me. I shall now burn myself in celestial fire." She then disappeared and a glow was seen travelling up into the sky.

The Venmani family has no male members now as cursed by the divine spirit but as predicted by her, two men from the last generation of males were great scholars. The Venmani Nambudiripads one hears of now are members of a branch which had detached itself from the main family a very long time ago and, therefore, did not come under the curse.

A Foreigner's Faith*

How a British functionary displayed faith in the deity of the royal family and was saved by divine intervention.

The Malayalam Era year 986 corresponding to our calendar year 1811 marked the demise of Balarama Varma Maharaja of Travancore leaving the royal family without a male descendant to succeed him. Therefore, as permitted by the British government, the seniormost woman member of the family, Maharani Lakshmi, took over the reins of government.

The British government then took a decision that a British representative would be appointed to run the government in any princely state which had no heir to the throne. This representative would continue till a male heir was born and reached the age of majority when he would take over the government. This decision was conveyed to all States through their Dewans or Prime Ministers appointed by the rulers with a request for a confirmation regarding the existence or otherwise of an heir in each of those States.

At that time, Travancore State had Mr. Munroe as both Dewan and British Resident. He did not respond to the letter from the British government. Maharani Lakshmi was expecting a child and Munroe decided to wait until the baby was born before sending a definite reply. This delay in replying did not please the British government which sent another letter to the Dewan demanding that a reply be sent immediately on receipt of the letter. This embarrassed the Dewan who was a British subject and really an employee of the British government. He thought that as the baby was expected in the next three or four days, ideally he should wait till then to send a response. However, that was obviously not possible.

Munroe proceeded to the eastern entrance of Shri Padmanabhaswami temple in Thiruvananthapuram and facing the west prayed to the deity,

*Oru Europeante Swaamibhakti

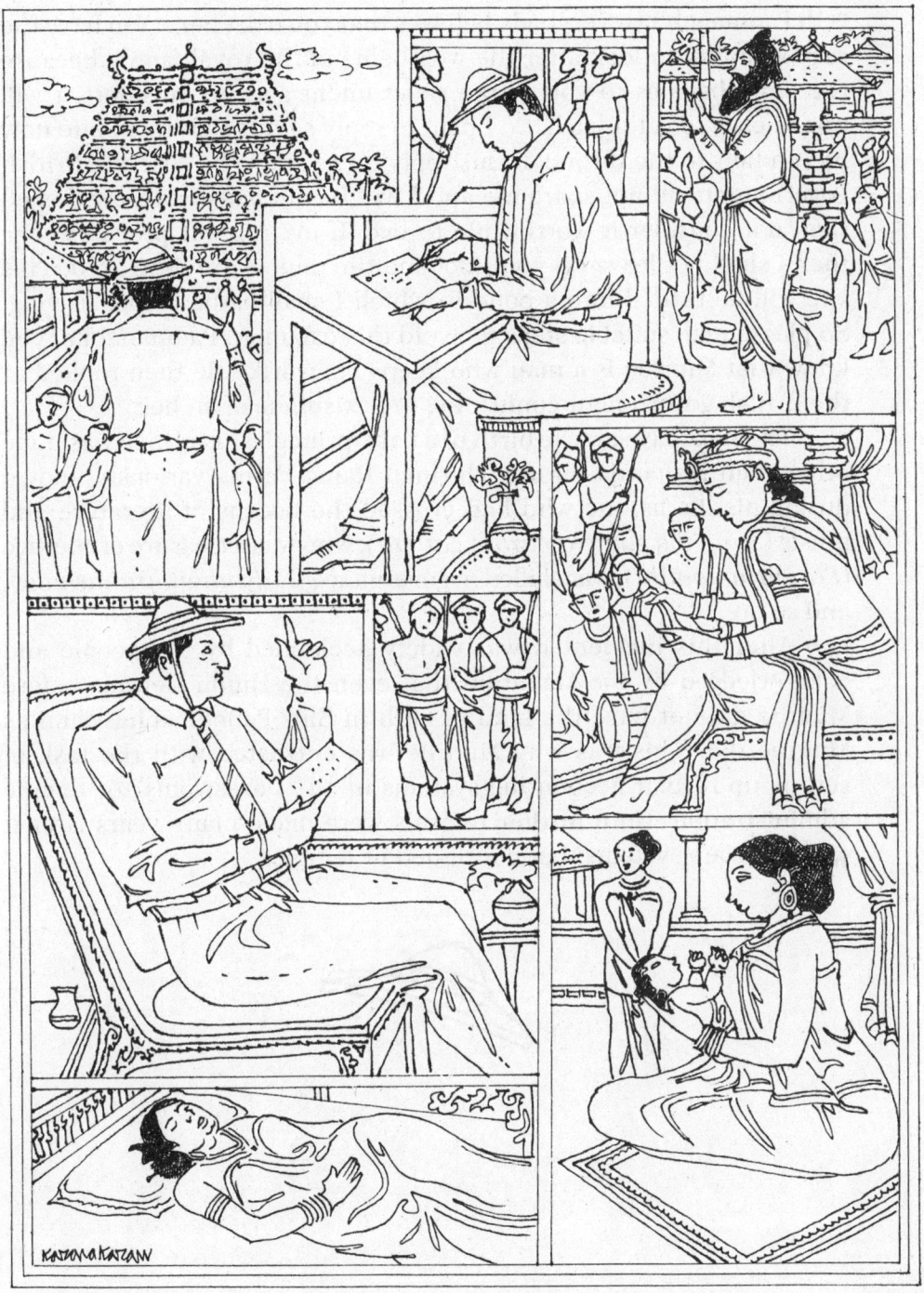

KATANAKATAAN

"Oh Padmanabha, everybody believes that you exist here. You have the responsibility to look after the well-being of the royal family because the State belongs to you. If the government goes to outsiders it will not be easy to get it back. So I plan to reply saying that this State now has an heir to the throne. If this reply turns out to be false the British government will not spare me and I will be punished severely. I shall then not consider it worthwhile to live. If my reply is proved wrong then I shall not leave till your idol and the temple are destroyed. This site will be turned into a pond in which I shall bathe before leaving. So please take suitable steps to avoid this calamity. Padmanabha, you know that Munroe is a man who keeps his word." He then replied to the British government confirming the existence of an heir.

The next day saw the birth of a baby prince! This prince was none other than Maharaja Swathi Thirunal Rama Varma variously known during his life as one who had crossed the oceans of literature and music (*Sangitha sahitya param gathah*), who was a treasure of courage (*Parakramanidhi*), was skilled in governance (*Rajyathanthrakushala*), and so on.

After this incident it was widely acclaimed by the people and acknowledged by the Maharani that even the Hindu Dewans before Munroe did not have the kind of faith in Shri Padmanabhaswami as Munroe did. This was why Munroe was entrusted with the task of setting up regular accounting systems in all "Devaswoms" or temple administration. Until further reforms were made many years later it was Munroe's systems that continued in temples.

The Hill Temple of Kerala*

The story below is of a deity of immense power and popularity who draws hundreds of thousands of pilgrims from around the country every year and many from outside as well.

 Long ago the Pandya royal family split into two and one group went to Madurai. The senior Raja from this group was out hunting and came across a young man who was also hunting. The Raja was so impressed with the bearing and hunting skill of the youth that he called him to his side and asked him who he was, where he came from, and such other questions. The reply was vague and went somewhat like this, "I don't belong anywhere except to the whole world. People call me Ayyappan. My father is a Malayali which makes me one too. I don't have parents in the normal sense. I exist in the belief that the goddess Mahamaya is my mother and the lord Ishwara is my father. I have nothing more to say." The ruler decided that this seemingly destitute lad was very skilled in the use of weapons and would, therefore, be a good addition to his army. He made this offer to Ayyappan who readily accepted it. Thus Ayyappan began his service with the Pandya ruler.

Those were days when there were frequent conflicts between kingdoms and the Pandya territory also was not immune to them. It turned out that in all these conflicts young Ayyappan came back victorious and soon he became the commander of the Pandya army. Ayyappan's mere presence halted attacks against the Pandya territory in course of time, a matter which sealed the bond of regard and affection that the ruler had for Ayyappan. This resulted in the old members of the army resenting Ayyappan and deciding to destroy him. They hit upon a plot for this purpose and secretly approached the queen.

The dissident soldiers complained to the queen that Ayyappan had turned the ruler against them. They were aggrieved that the ruler did

---

*Shabarimala Shaasthaavum Panthalam Rajaavum

not trust them with any mission and even appeared to disapprove of them. Thus they had decided that if a solution could not be found they would have to leave the ruler's service. The queen was sympathetic and suggested that they return to her after they had finalized a plan. The queen assured them that she would help implement that plan. Very soon the soldiers were back with the plan that the queen should feign illness which would not respond to any treatment that would be given by the local physicians. The next part of the plan would be implemented by the soldiers.

The queen accordingly pretended to fall victim to an unknown illness which seemed to resist the treatment of all the well-known doctors who were summoned. Matters got desperate when the queen's condition appeared to worsen and at this crucial stage the old soldiers sent a hireling pretending to be a physician. He gave a frightening diagnosis and suggested that the only known remedy was three measures of tiger's milk which had to be procured from the forest. It was suggested that in order to ensure the success of this dangerous mission none other than Ayyappan should venture into the forest. Ayyappan was thus instructed to try and bring back three measures of tiger's milk. The plotters were sure that he would be killed in the attempt.

Ayyappan went into the forest, located and herded together a number of tigresses and cubs. He returned to the palace riding a tigress and followed by several of the other tigers. Seeing this there was panic in the palace with everyone including the old soldiers scurrying for hiding places. One look at the animals was enough to cure the queen fully. The ruler realized that Ayyappan was no simple mortal. He fell at Ayyappan's feet pleading for forgiveness for treating Ayyappan as an employee and begging that the wild animals be sent back into the forest. Ayyappan assured the ruler that there was no reason for apology and that he was happy over the way the ruler had treated him. He revealed to the ruler that it was all a plot hatched by the jealous soldiers.

Ayyappan conveyed to the ruler his decision to go back to his roots in Kerala and advised the ruler also to follow him. The ruler was deeply affected by Ayyappan's disappearance from his court.

The ruler struggled to establish Ayyappan's identity. He pondered over the vague self-introduction that Ayyappan had given. His father was Lord Ishwara and his mother Goddess Mahamaya. Could Ayyappan then

be Shastha, son born to Shiva and Vishnu in his disguise as Mahamaya? He cursed himself for not realising this earlier and resolved to follow Ayyappan to Kerala with his family.

The Raja leased out his property, collected his money, jewellery, and such other movable items and commenced his journey. He finally reached a place called Panthalam which, at that time, was in the control of an aristocrat named "Kaipuzha Thamban" from whom he bought some land. He built a palace on this land and lived there with his family eventually coming to be known as Panthalam Raja.

"Kaipuzha Thamban" was famed for his magical powers but over the years his family faded away and Panthalam Raja shifted his palace to the Kaipuzha part of Panthalam. His palace was located on the banks of a beautiful and full river.

Meanwhile, Ayyappan had travelled towards Kerala and at its eastern border happened to meet the famous sage Parasurama. The latter said to Ayyappan, "Oh, son of Lord Shiva, I have already established your idols on the mountains on the eastern border of Kerala and the seashore on the west. I now propose to establish another idol at this holy spot where we have met. Your presence is needed in all these locations. It is here that eminent sages such as Matanga Maharshi spent their lives in prayer. It is here that Shabari spent her life in the service of these sages and was eventually given moksha (salvation) by Lord Rama. I consider you the protector of Kerala and that your presence in this holy spot is of special importance." Ayyappan agreed and his idol was established there and that mountain where Shabari lived and attained moksha was named Shabarimala or Shabari mountain.

One night Panthalam Raja dreamt that his former commander Ayyappan visited him and said, "I live on Shabarimala and you can see me if you go there." The Raja headed for Shabarimala the next day with his retinue. He reached Shabarimala and set about clearing the jungle when he saw the Ayyappa idol that the sage Parasurama had established. He was disappointed that he did not see Ayyappa in person but then a voice was heard saying, "Please be satisfied with seeing my idol now. If you worship that idol all your desires will be fulfilled." The Raja recognised Ayyappan's voice and immediately made arrangements to stay there and oversee the construction of a temple around the idol. The temple was consecrated by a well-known priest who also laid down the schedule of rituals to be observed in the temple.

As wild animals roamed the forest and it was impossible for people to stay in the temple for any considerable length of time it was decided that worship in the temple would be limited to five days in the month. The first day of the Malayalam month of *Makaram* (December/January) would be specially celebrated every year and thereafter there would be a festival for five days beginning with that day. There would also be special worship on the seventh day of Makaram. It has since been the practice to observe the rituals in the temple during the first five days of six alternate months and during the last five days of the other six alternate months. This was to reduce travel through inhospitable terrain to six rather than twelve times a year. The priests, attendants, and others walked through the forest carrying on their heads bundles containing rice, provisions, and other items for the rituals. As they walked they vociferously invoked Ayyappan's mercy *"Swamiye Sharanam Ayyappa!"* or ("Oh Ayyappan, protect us!"). The wild animals always gave them safe passage.

When Panthalam Raja returned home he accepted Ayyappan as his principal deity. A temple was built next to the palace so that the Raja could worship Ayyappan every day and this temple was thrown open to all devotees.

It may be recalled that the Pandya royal family split and one group went to Madurai. The other group had been living in Valliyur. In course of time this group also moved to Kerala and reached a place called Poonjar in Thekkumkur in what is currently Meenachel taluk in Travancore. They bought land from the local ruler and built a palace for themselves. They also accepted Ayyappan as their family deity and built a temple near the palace where rituals and festivals became a normal routine.

After annexing Thekkumkur, Vadakkumkur, Kayamkulam, and such principalities, the Maharaja of Travancore wished to add Panthalam also to his State. This he did without a war by means of a treaty which guaranteed the Panthalam family total protection, an annual pension, and paddy and funds for their daily living. With the normal increase in the size of the family and without a proportionate enhancement of financial and other support, one can imagine the difficult circumstances of the Panthalam family over a period of years.

Even after Panthalam became part of Travancore the Shabarimala temple remained outside State control. However, over time, when the income of the temple increased, the State took over the running of the temple as well thus depriving the Panthalam Raja of any benefit from the temple which he had built and managed. The Raja, however, continued to be the custodian of the temple ornaments and jewellery. It is still his privilege to carry these ornaments and jewellery every year to reach Shabarimala temple in time for the rituals on the first day of Makaram. This journey is undertaken with much ceremony with an escort of police and government officials and to the accompaniment of drums, pipes, and such other traditional musical instruments. The expenses of this procession and the stay of the Panthalam Raja for seven days in Shabarimala are borne by the State.

Despite the Panthalam Raja's close connection with the Shabarimala temple he does not by tradition stand directly in front of the idol for worship. Two reasons were suggested for this. One was that he did not wish to inconvenience Ayyappan who may feel compelled to rise to show respect for his former employer. The other was attributed to the possible rivalry between the Panthalam Raja from the warrior caste of kshatriyas and the sage Parasurama who established the idol.

Although the main deity in Shabarimala is Ayyappan there are three other deities who are also worshipped there. One is the goddess Kali who sits on the top floor of a two-storeyed building. Then there are Vaavar, a Muslim, and Kaduthaswami from a low caste who are also revered as close devotees of Ayyappan. The rituals on the seventh day of Makaram are dedicated to these three deities.

Much is known about the power that Ayyappan wields to this day and the miracles He has performed. However this is not being repeated here as there is enough proof on record and in actual experience.

Sanghakkali –
An Ancient Dance Form*

How a vigorous group dance which originated as a means of prayer for winning a competition, came to be practised later as a religious rite for the fulfilment of one's desires.

Sanghakkali is a dance form performed not for entertainment but as part of religious rituals related to events such as a baby's introduction to a meal of rice (*annapraasham*), the sacred thread ceremony (*upanayanam*), weddings, and so on. A Sanghakkali performance is also offered to God together with a request for a boon, say for a child, or as thanksgiving for a favour granted. Unlike other offerings which are made by oneself the offer of Sanghakkali has to be made through groups specially designated for this. These groups have to be fed liberally, given gifts, and then they lead a prayer which is repeated by the person who is making the request to God. There are numerous first-hand reports of desires being expressed, the promise of Sanghakkali being made to God and such a performance being conducted lavishly on the desire being fulfilled by divine grace. However, the origin of Sanghakkali is hardly known and given below is the history of how Sanghakkali came into existence.

It is well known that in the olden days Kerala was ruled by a succession of Perumal kings who came from outside the region. One of them embraced Islam and at the instance of Muslim leaders summoned Malayali Brahmins from sixty-four villages and insisted that they too should embrace Islam. This led to a debate on which was a better religion, and to put an end to this, the king said he would set a test and the religion of whichever side passed this test would prevail. The Brahmins agreed but requested that the test be held after forty-five days. This was conceded.

_____

Sanghakkali

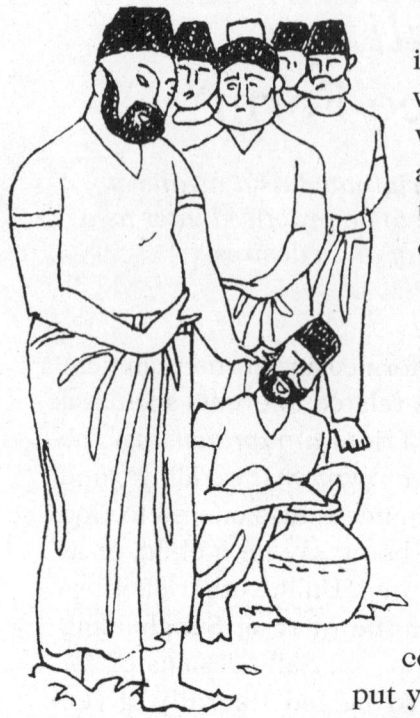

The Brahmins had agreed to the test in the absence of any option and on their way back from their meeting with the king were agonizing over their future course of action. Finally they surrendered their fate to the will of God. As they were returning they came across a saintly person who addressed them with these words, "Do not be afraid. I shall teach you a mantra (a magic verse). I advise you to go to Thrikkariyur temple, light a lamp there, worship there for forty-one days, circambulating the lamp, and repeating the verse. When you go back to the king you will see a sealed earthenware vessel and you will be asked to identify the contents. The Muslims will say it contains a venomous cobra and you have to say it contains a lotus flower. You will be asked to put your hand into the vessel and produce the contents for scrutiny. You may do this without fear. The king and his followers would have put a cobra into the vessel but it will turn into a lotus flower." The Brahmins realized that this person was no ordinary mortal and followed his instructions meticulously.

The day of the test arrived and the Brahmins presented themselves before the king, fresh from their worship in Thrikkariyur temple. What followed was exactly as the stranger had predicted. When the Brahmins were asked to produce the contents of the vessel for all to witness the king and his Muslim followers expected to see the Brahmin representative succumbing to the bite of the cobra. However, the lotus flower emerged much to the dismay of the king and the others. The Muslims left in embarrassment while the Brahmins were seen off showered with suitable honours.

On their way back after the test they met the stranger again at whose feet they prostrated. He advised them thus, "Hereafter the verse I have taught you is to be used for the good of others. Those who have unfulfilled desires should be asked to light a lamp and circumambulate it repeating the verse. You must also keep this verse alive by passing

it down to your succeeding generations." Having said this the stranger vanished. All these events soon became public knowledge and the Brahmins were besieged by those wishing to benefit from their experience.

Sanghakkali commences with the lighting of the lamp after which the group goes round the lamp repeating the magic verse loudly, very slowly and in a particular range of tones. It is said that the stranger was the famous sage Narada. Very soon the Brahmins found that they could not cope with the persistent demand for their services and they then split into eighteen groups, each dealing with its own list of client families. Some of the larger families enlisted the services of more than one group while local rulers often asked for all eighteen groups to perform Sanghakkali for them.

Before the time of the Perumal kings some of the Malayali Brahmins had trained in the use of arms for the defence of their territory and such Brahmins were not permitted the usual access to the Hindu scriptures. When the Brahmins were in Thrikkariyur temple prior to the king's test the armed Brahmins had accompanied them as escorts. These latter occupied themselves by singing and dancing in various costumes. In course of time such songs and dancing became popular with the people and came to be accepted as part of the Sanghakkali ritual.

It is the armed Brahmins who play an important role in the Sanghakkali performance. There are two sections, both of which participate in Sanghakkali, but only one of which is preferred for the performance as well as for cooking the feast which follows. The *sangham* or group is not complete unless it includes at least two Brahmins well versed in the scriptures.

Interest and belief in rituals such as Sanghakkali have waned in recent years and one has to accept that this is inevitable in the newly developing environment.

The Chinese Jars and the Mango Pickle*

This is the story of a Chinese shipwreck, of how honesty was rewarded in a strange way and how it led to an unexpected ending.

The Pandanparambath Bhattathiri family lived in the erstwhile British Malabar part of Kerala and at one time was very poor. It was at that time that a Chinese trader set out with a shipload of costly cargo. Midway, the ship was wrecked and most of the cargo and all the crew were lost in the disaster. The trader managed to reach the shore in a boat with just ten Chinese jars and stumbled upon Bhattathiri's home which was an old and dilapidated building.

The trader stood outside the building and shouted, "Is anybody at home?" The Bhattathiri family was on the point of beginning a frugal meal of rice gruel. On hearing the shout Bhattathiri came out and the Chinese trader described his shipwreck and the depth of his hunger. Taking pity on him Bhattathiri gave him the rice gruel which was consumed eagerly. Thereafter the trader said, "Please do not think you have just given me a meal. You have saved my life and I can never forget the taste of the gruel. At present I cannot give you a suitable reward but on my next visit I hope to be able to make up for this. Meanwhile I request you to keep these ten Chinese jars till I return. They contain nothing valuable, just lentils." Bhattathiri agreed and the trader departed leaving the jars sealed and secured.

Some days passed and one day it so happened that the Bhattathiri family had no means of cooking their next meal. The couple and their children were famished and the wife suggested that they might consider opening one of the jars and using some of the lentils contained in it. After much discussion about the ethics of taking someone else's property without his permission they were finally persuaded by the sheer despair

---

*Pandanparambathu Kotanbharaniyile Uppumanga

of hunger. Bhattathiri opened one jar and put his hand in to take out some lentils. He found that the contents were not only lentils and so he brought the jar out into the light. They were taken aback by what they saw. The jar was filled with gold coins which were covered by a thin layer of lentils. The other nine jars were no different. So Bhattathiri took out one gold coin from a jar, sealed all the jars again and put them away. He sold the gold coin and with the money bought rice and other provisions with which the entire family had a hearty meal.

Bhattathiri then began to wonder why he should not use some of the gold coins to improve his life style. With the trader on his way back to China Bhattathiri would be able to replace the coins before the trader returned. He took the gold coins and using them he built himself a huge mansion and bought much land and all that was required for a comfortable life. His investment soon began to fetch him a good return with which he proceeded to replace the coins he had taken from the jars. In seven or eight years he filled all the jars as before and in addition filled ten half-size jars with gold coins all of which he stored away safely.

It was twelve years before the Chinese trader returned with another shipload. He came searching for Bhattathiripad's house but could find no trace of it. On enquiry he was told by those in the area that the mansion belonged to Bhattathiri who had discovered a treasure which transformed his life. The trader suspected that the treasure must have been the ten jars and that all the contents may have been used up. He went to the mansion and was soon received warmly by Bhattathiri. The trader and his crew were treated to a lavish meal after which Bhattathiri and the trader sat down for a chat. Bhattathiri told the trader truthfully about how poverty and hunger had forced him to open the jars and how he had used the contents thereafter to improve his life. He apologized for his unauthorized use of the coins and assured him that all the coins had been replaced and that another ten half-size jars had also been filled with coins as interest on the coins used. Saying this the twenty jars were produced before the trader. The trader refused to take the small jars saying that he owed Bhattathiri money for storing the jars and that he would not accept the interest. Bhattathiri pleaded with the trader that he should take the small jars at least as an atonement from him for taking the trader's money without permission. The trader refused

to change his mind saying that if Bhattathiri's life style had changed it was due to his initiative. The trader's money had been kept safe and that was all that he intended to take. He insisted that the ten small jars be put away in storage after which he gave Bhattathiri one of the big jars as a traditional offering to a Brahmin with an accompaniment of flowers and such other items.

Before leaving, the trader informed Bhattathiri that the Chinese jars were lucky and where they stayed there would be no poverty or want. He also said that pickled mango stored in the jars would acquire an unique taste which could not be created in any other way. The trader then took his nine jars and left. Bhattathiri emptied the contents of the eleven jars into another vessel and it is said that the eleven are still stored safely.

Bhattathiri began to pickle mangoes and store them in the Chinese jar and these soon became famous all around. The mango pickle remained ever fresh in the jar and was considered to be a sure remedy for loss of appetite.

There is a story about how much in demand the mango pickle stored in the Chinese jar went on to be. There was a feast arranged by a Maharaja for very eminent Nambudiris and after dinner they were discussing the high quality of the food that was served. One of them said, "The food was magnificent and there cannot be another meal like this." Another Nambudiri responded, "No doubt this meal was superb but a bit of that Pandanparambathu pickle would have made a huge difference." The Maharaja overheard this conversation and secretly sent for that pickle which he served at dinner the next night. Without knowing this the same Nambudiris tasted the pickle and had no difficulty in identifying it to be the pickle stored in the Chinese jar. Such was the uniqueness of the Chinese jar which, we are told, is still used to make that famed mango pickle.

Divine Protection,
Divine Justice*

*How intense devotion to goddess Shakthi protected Her devotee
but could not prevent Her from punishing him when he
presumed too much.*

He was a good Brahmin and a devotee of Shakthi. He worshipped Devi every single day. Besides this, on Tuesdays, Fridays, and New Moon days, as prescribed by tradition, he worshipped Shakthi with offerings of liquor and meat. After the worship he drank the offering of liquor. Devi was his visible goddess.

It was well known to other Brahmins that Puliambilly Nambudiri worshipped Shakthi and consumed liquor. However, because of his acknowledged divinity nobody was able to investigate it too closely or declare him an outcast. Whenever he was not present, the other Nambudiris used to discuss him, "He is a base individual and is what he does appropriate for a Brahmin? We should not invite this drunkard to any occasion in our homes. If he comes without an invitation we should throw him out. We should also refuse to visit his home for any occasion." It so happened that nobody was willing to confront him on these lines. How could he be excommunicated without a valid reason? So all the local Nambudiris lay in wait for a suitable reason and time.

On a certain Friday the Nambudiris learnt that Puliambilly Nambudiri had gone to buy liquor for his Shakthi worship. They decided to confront him on his way back with the liquor and accordingly waited in hiding. Very soon he was sighted returning with the pot of liquor on his head. All the Nambudiris emerged from hiding and surrounded him. Sure of their success they asked him what the pot contained. Puliambilly Nambudiri realized that they were out to get him. As he was confident that they could do him no harm he decided to egg them on in their effort. He pretended to be nervous and evasive which encouraged the

*Puliambilly Namboori

Nambudiris. They all asked him with redoubled vigour, "What is in that pot?" He looked embarrassed and with bowed head he replied softly, "There is nothing much in this pot." Then some of the Nambudiris insisted on examining the contents of the pot and grabbed it. The smell of liquor hit them confirming their suspicion regarding the contents. The Nambudiris insisted that the pot be opened to which Puliambilly responded, "It contains treated arecanut for my wife for use with her betel leaf." A demand that the arecanut be shown followed and the more Puliambilly hesitated the more vigorous became the demand. So Puliambilly agreed to open the pot and when the contents were shown to the Nambudiris they happened to be arecanut treated in a traditional way! It is easy to imagine the embarrassment of the Nambudiris. When they had all dispersed Puliambilly closed the pot and made his way home. When the pot was opened for worship the contents had turned into liquor again.

Thus despite many attempts the Nambudiris were unable to find proof that Puliambilly consumed liquor. The worship and the consumption of the liquor offering were indoors and at night. During this time visitors were turned away by the servants with instructions to return the next morning. So how could anyone insist on seeing Puliambilly after he had retired for the night? The next day saw Puliambilly showing no signs of having consumed any liquor.

The Nambudiris were greatly frustrated for a long time and finally informed the local ruler who ordered that the day of the next worship be communicated to him. He would then find a way to verify the complaint. They soon received word that the next Shakthi worship would be on New Moon day in the Malayalam month of *Karkidagom* and the information was promptly relayed to the ruler. As Puliambilly was resting after the worship and partaking of the offering of liquor he was summoned by the ruler. The message from the ruler was conveyed to the maid servant who informed Puliambilly's wife who in turn relayed it to Puliambilly himself who was at that time resting in an alcoholic daze. He said the ruler should be informed that the night was too dark and he would start as soon as the moon had risen.

Meanwhile a huge gathering of Nambudiris had

assembled in the ruler's presence hoping to catch Puliambilly red-handed and have him excommunicated. The messenger returned with the message that Puliambilly would be on his way as soon as the moon rose. Hearing this the Nambudiris were convinced that Puliambilly was under the influence of alcohol as there was no possibility of the moon rising on a New Moon night. As it was late into the night the Nambudiris did not go back to their homes. When the ruler had retired for the night the Nambudiris dispersed to sleep in various corners of the palace.

Towards midnight Puliambilly recovered from the effects of liquor and remembered as if in a dream that he had sent a foolish response to the ruler. He confirmed this with his wife and suffered much embarrassment.

Confident of the blessing of Shakthi, the Universal Mother, and her protection from harm he got up and set off for the palace. He suddenly realized that the moon had risen in the sky and was shedding its light everywhere. Pleased with this he soon reached the palace and knocked at the door of the royal bedchamber and disclosed his identity. "Has the moon risen?" was the ruler's question. "Yes, if you step outside you will see it," responded Puliambilly. The ruler stepped out of his bedchamber and was surprised to see the moon. He immediately had all the Nambudiris summoned and they, needless to say, could not believe their eyes. The ruler showered gifts on Puliambilly and sent him home. As soon as Puliambilly reached his house the moonlight disappeared. The moonlight was not real, of course. The goddess, Shakthi, ever concerned with the well-being of her devotees, was anxious to protect Puliambilly and had taken off one of her ear-rings and held it against the sky. It gave everybody the impression that the moon had risen and was shedding its brightness everywhere. Thus all attempts made by many to humiliate Puliambilly, to publicize his use of liquor, and have him excommunicated ended in failure. It is, of course, well known that it is impossible to harm one who has divine blessing.

Puliambilly was an expert in magic and his services were much in demand. There were no evil spirits that could not be exorcised by him. Whenever he travelled the goddess Shakthi went with him as a visible companion but She was invisible to others.

It was midnight once when he was returning after an assignment. He was walking ahead with the goddess behind him. At one point when he looked back he did not see Her. He stopped a while wondering where she could have gone and was filled with concern. When She did not return he decided to turn back and search for Her. When he had gone some distance he saw a pariah hovel of one of untouchable caste, where the goddess Shakthi was seated on a stool with a sword by her side. The pariah was singing Her praises and drumming while She appeared to be acknowledging his worship although she was invisible to him. Puliambilly waited until the worship had ended. When Shakthi rose to return to Puliambilly he said, "My goddess, it is inappropriate that you should enter a pariah's hut. I was hurt to see that you not only acknowledged the worship of a lowly pariah ignorant of rituals but you also partook of his offering of food. I beseech you to please desist from such acts at least in future." Hearing this the goddess smiled and said "Oh, so you have not understood me well till now. You do not yet have enough purity of mind and devotion. For me all my devotees are equal. There is no difference between Brahmin and pariah. I cannot refuse to answer the call of anyone who is devoted to me. I value devotion more than knowledge of rituals. I shall not henceforth accompany one who does not seem to know this truth. I shall also cease to be visible to you. However, if you continue to worship me I shall enable you to realize your desires." Thereafter She disappeared and was never again visible to him. He did not live long after that.

Puliambilly Nambudiri is still worshipped in many places in Kerala as a family deity. There is a ritual in the Malayalam months of Karkidagom and *Thulam* in which an offering of water is made to him. It is believed that this offering enables the fulfilment of one's desires ranging from acquiring wealth and having children to the elimination of evil spirits. Solving cases of theft is one of the important powers of this offering of water. It is widely believed that within forty-one days of the offering being promised the thief would be forced to return the stolen goods and fall at the feet of the one he had robbed. Failing this the thief and his family would all vomit blood and die. The same fate is said to befall one who promises but does not make the offering.

Puliambilly is reputed to be one of the most feared deities with a quality that resembles the famous two-edged sword of Kayamkulam.

Puliambilly's home was in Kozhikode in Kerala and he died over five centuries ago. It has to be assumed that if he is revered by people even in current times he must have possessed great divinity and been capable of working miracles during his lifetime.

The Mango of Eternal Life*

*How a magic mango supposed to give eternal life
threatened instead to bring eternal strife.*

There are two versions of the life of the famous philosopher-
poet-king Bharthruhari. One says he was always a *brahmachari*
(celibate) while the other version is that he had a wife but that
he gave up family life out of frustration and despair. A story
which supports the second version is narrated below.

An ascetic once gave Bharthruhari a mango and
said that the one who ate the mango would live for ever.
Bharthruhari thought over the matter and decided there
was no point in his outliving his wife whom he truly loved.
He, therefore, gave it to his wife and explained the power
of the mango. The wife who was believed by Bharthruhari
to be faithful and devoted to him had a lover who was
none other than the caretaker of Bharthruhari's horses.
The wife had no desire to live after her lover had died and
so gave her lover the mango with a suitable introduction
to its magical power. This lover passed on the mango to
his wife so that she could live after he had died. This
woman was the maid in Bharthruhari's residence and as
she was leaving for her home with the mango in her hand she passed
Bharthruhari on the way.

Bharthruhari noticed and recognised the mango and stopped the
maid to find out how she had come to possess the mango. She said
that her husband had given it to her. Bharthruhari returned home and
questioned his horseman who, after trying to deceive his master with
lies, finally confessed to his relationship with Bharthruhari's wife and
how he had received the mango from her. Bharthruhari was distraught
over the deceit practised by his wife whom he had trusted and loved.
However, he decided to say nothing about it. Bharthruhari's wife heard

---

*Bharthruhari

from her lover that they had been found out and she decided that her husband had to be eliminated. She prepared a sweetmeat laced with poison and offered it to her husband saying the next meal would be delayed and that he should have a snack in the meantime.

Bharthruhari suspected that his wife would plot against his life and made up his mind to leave her. He decided to give up his worldly ties and become a *sanyasin* or ascetic. He took an earthen pot in his hand, dropped the sweetmeat in his home, and departed. The moment he left, his house burst into flames.

Bharthruhari wandered around as an ascetic not asking for alms but living on charity offered to him. He finally came to a large temple (presumed to be Chidambaram in Tamil Nadu). At the eastern entrance of the temple was a sage by the name of Pattanathu Pillai and so Bharthruhari sat at the western entrance with the pot in front of him. He ate if food was dropped in his pot and starved if it was not. However, he was not affected by the erratic food habits. One day a beggar approached Pattanathu Pillai and asked for alms. Pattanathu Pillai said he had nothing to offer and said there was a rich man sitting at the other entrance who would probably be able to help. The beggar went to Bharthruhari for alms but Bharthruhari told him that he was himself a beggar. On reflection Bharthruhari decided that his possession of a pot was what made him out to be wealthier than Pattanathu Pillai and that it could give the impression he was asking for alms. The pot was promptly discarded. The legend is that Bharthruhari sat there during the rest of his years and that his more famous verses were composed during that time.

The Mango of Eternal Life

The Temple of the Snakes*

*Most temples have strange origins. Our story illustrates this fact
and shows the kind of belief that is generated
regardless of caste.*

Parasurama founded Kerala and then invited many Brahmins
from outside Kerala to move into the region. However, the
area was infested by serpents and besides, there was not a
drop of pure water to be had. Therefore, they decided to
return to whence they came. Parasurama was disappointed
and approached his mentor, Lord Shiva on Mount Kailasa,
who was all-knowing and had a serpent as his necklace. Lord
Shiva advised Parasurama to pray to Vasuki, the serpent king,
and seek his help.

Parasurama went back to Kerala and commenced his single-minded
meditation to obtain Vasuki's assistance. Vasuki did appear before him
and in response to Parasurama's petition Vasuki assured him that both
problems, related to serpents and impure water, would be dealt with.
However, Vasuki suggested that the serpents had to be treated with
respect and temples had to be built in different parts of Kerala where
the serpents of those different areas could find shelter and be revered.
The saline water would all be diverted to the sea and pure water would
be available for the inhabitants.

Parasurama promptly set about re-inviting the Brahmins to return
to Kerala. The water became potable and the serpents withdrew into the
forests till the temples were built providing shelter for them. Parasurama
cleared a large area of the jungle where he had prayed to Vasuki and
established Vasuki and his followers as the local deities. People began to
live in that area and worship commenced on a regular scale. A Brahmin
family, now known as Mannarshala Nambiathiris, was designated to
manage the Vasuki temple.

The origin of the name Mannarshala has an interesting story
attached to it. When one of the Pandavas of Mahabharatha, Arjuna, set

---

*The Mannaarshaala Maahaatmyam

fire to the Khandava forest (now Ambalapuzha) this fire spread to the neighbourhood of the Vasuki temple. The women of the Nambiathiri family tried to prevent the fire from spreading further by dousing the area with water from the nearby lake. While the temple was saved the soil became very hot and the serpents were in danger. The women, however, continued to pour water all around until the people shouted, "*Mannu aari*" or "The soil (*mannu*) has cooled (*aari*)." It was then agreed that the place should be called "Mannu aari shala" or "Mannarshala."

There are many interesting and incredible experiences attached to the Mannarshala temple. It is customary for serpents to be offered milk to which rice flour and turmeric are added. After the rituals the vessels are emptied and placed upside down. In Mannarshala this is not done and the vessels and contents are left untouched. The temple door is locked and it is said that when the temple is opened the next morning the vessels are always empty.

It was never the practice in Mannarshala Nambiathiri's house to put away and lock up the various possessions of the family. Even vegetables which grew in plenty on the vast property were safe. The serpents guarded the property all the time. There is a story of a person who stole a pumpkin from the Mannarshala yard. When the pumpkin was cut open there was a serpent inside. The thief immediately recognized the reason and pleaded with the serpent to forgive him. He promised to atone for his sin and placed ten coins at the temple door before the serpent disappeared from the scene.

There was also a Nair family which visited the temple for a long stay to worship there. They had brought their own rice and provisions with which to cook their food but borrowed a measuring vessel for the rice. After their stay they packed up their belongings and entirely by mistake, packed the measuring vessel in the rice sack. When the sack was opened and emptied they discovered the measuring vessel and coiled inside it was a serpent. Here again a promise of atonement was made and the serpent disappeared.

Not far from Mannarshala in Thakazhi there was a family with a yard full of trees. One of them was a jackfruit tree which never bore fruit despite its mature years. The head of the family was advised to offer the first fruit to Mannarshala temple. Nothing happened for a while

and the fruiting season had ended by then. Then more in jest he raised his offer to twin fruits rather than single ones. Lo and behold, although the jackfruit season was over the tree bore twin fruits in plenty! All these were sent to Mannarshala in boats and thereafter the tree began to bear fruit regularly and needless to say, the first fruits went to the temple every time.

There are many reports of the temple bringing relief to people beset with problems of many kinds. There were many who stayed in the temple for days in worship, seeking a cure for serious diseases and for exorcising evil spirits. There are even instances of childless women of forty-five years and more having their prayer for children answered. The devotees include many non-Hindus.

The *Ayilyam* day in the Malayalam month of *Kanni* (roughly September/October) is celebrated in Mannarshala temple with special rituals, processions, and so on. The Maharaja of Travancore who reigned in the late years of the eighteenth century used to attend these celebrations regularly but there was one year in which he had to attend to urgent business elsewhere on that day. He was very disappointed and ordered that similar celebrations should be held at his expense on the same day in the following month. This was done and soon became a regular practice.

There have been some interesting experiences that have been reported very recently by those who have read this Mannarshala story. A Christian in Kottayam has written to say that a jackfruit tree in his compound had not produced a single fruit for quite a few years. After reading this description of Mannarshala temple he offered to send the first fruit from that tree to the temple. Very soon four or five fruits appeared on the tree. His dilemma was how to send the fruit to the temple without being noticed by other Christians who would make fun of his faith. I have advised him to ascertain the market value of the fruits and send an equivalent amount with an explanatory letter to Mannarshala Nambiathiri who would do whatever is appropriate with it. I have also informed him that there are Muslims and other Christians who are secretly doing the same.

Reading the Future*

This is the story of two reputed astrologers who could foretell the future by reading nature's signals.

In the Mangalapilly family in Aranmula in Travancore there was once a reputed and erudite astrologer known as Mangalapilly Moothathu. Not far away was a close friend and another eminent astrologer, Samprathi Pillai.

On one occasion Moothathu decided to visit his friend Pillai on his way on some work. It so happened that at the same time a Nambudiri visited Pillai with a number of women's horoscopes from which he wished to have one chosen for marriage. Moothathu was received with warmth and respect and after the preliminary greeting was over Pillai suggested to Moothathu that they both scrutinize the horoscopes and thus save time. They could then converse at leisure.

Moothathu merely looked at the horoscopes and rejected them one by one until he was able to pick one. He then declared, "This horoscope is a good match according to astrological science but then he will not get her hand in marriage." The Nambudiri then looked at that horoscope and said, "If this horoscope is a good match I will get this girl. Her family and mine are known to each other very well." Moothathu then responded, "Do go and try but the result will be as I have predicted. You will marry another girl but even that marriage will not work as she will die soon after. If you want to have children you will have to marry yet again." The client refused to believe the prediction and left determined to pursue the chosen horoscope.

The Nambudiri approached the girl's family who agreed readily to the marriage. Preparations were made for the wedding and the date and time fixed. A distinguished group of guests was invited and on the day of the ceremony everything was in readiness. Unfortunately the members of the families assembled there had a disagreement which grew into a conflict. Eventually one group threatened to boycott the ceremony if

---

Mangalapilli Moothathum and Punnayil Panikkarum

it went through while the other was ready to walk out if the marriage did not take place. The father of the bride was in a dilemma and asked the two sides to arrive at a solution. One of the guests opposing the marriage offered himself as the bridegroom without any demand for dowry. The father accepted this solution and the girl was married to the new bridegroom. The Nambudiri was totally dejected by the turn of events till someone from the other camp went to him and offered his daughter in marriage with double the original dowry. Thus both the marriages took place in the same auspicious period. However, in six months the Nambudiri lost his wife. He was greatly impressed by Moothathu's prediction and decided to go to him again with some horoscopes from which to choose a new bride.

When the Nambudiri reached Moothathu's house, the latter was away in the local temple. He returned soon and on seeing the Nambudiri he opened the conversation, "Well, things happened as I had predicted, didn't they? Now you wish to marry again, don't you?" The Nambudiri conceded that Moothathu was correct in his assumptions and requested that the right choice be made from the horoscopes he had taken with him. Moothathu replied, "I do not study horoscopes. I have an instinct which guides me and by God's grace my predictions never go wrong. As for selecting a horoscope for you, all you have to do is to choose two and discard them. The third will be the right one. It will be a lady born under the star *Karthika* and you may marry her without hesitation. She will give you two sons and a daughter. There will then be an abortion and no children thereafter. You may go now."

The Nambudiri followed Moothathu's advice and his married life progressed over the years as predicted. He was most impressed by Moothathu's accuracy. He went with his family to worship in the Aranmula temple and then called on Moothathu. A lavish feast had been arranged by the Nambudiri for Moothathu who was also generously rewarded.

In the past Kerala had several astrologers like Moothathu who made their predictions based on signals given by various natural sources in the environment. They needed no equipment or accessories for their predictions and depended entirely on the signs conveyed by natural "messengers".

Punnayil was a "Sudra" (lowest of the four varnas or castes) family near Kumaranellur which boasted of a reputed and erudite astrologer among its members who were known as "Punnayil Panikkars". It so happened that a Nambudiri in that area wished to fix the date and time for the sacred thread ceremony of his son. He consulted many astrologers but none of them were able to prescribe a suitable date and time. Finally he visited Punnayil Panikkar to seek his help and without any hesitation he wrote out a suitable day and hour for the ceremony. The Nambudiri took this advice to the other astrologers and questioned their expertise. These astrologers discovered that the prescribed time was inauspicious and challenged Panikkar's findings. There was much competition and jealousy among the astrologers and, thanks to his success, Panikkar was their main target. Panikkar was summoned and asked how he could prescribe that day and time which were not auspicious for the ceremony. Panikkar explained, "I agree that the day and hour prescribed by me are inauspicious. However, I find that the boy should complete the ceremony this year and this was the only day that was the least unsuitable." On being asked why the boy could not wait till the next year, Panikkar continued, "Next year the boy cannot have the ceremony as he will be observing the funeral rites of his mother. The following year has no suitable day at all and the year after he will be performing rituals connected with his father's death. Thus three years will pass and so will the age prescribed for the ceremony. Thereafter he will cease to be a Brahmin and can traditionally be ostracized." The astrologers had to agree that under the circumstances Panikkar was justified in prescribing as he had done. Events followed as Panikkar had predicted and jealousy and rivalry turned into respect and admiration for Panikkar.

The Raja's Dream Temple*

This is a narrative on the strange origin of a famous temple.

The Thirunakkara temple in Kottayam town in Travancore is well known to most people. One of the interesting legends about the Shiva idol and the bull of that temple is narrated below.

There was once a ruler of Thekkumkur who worshipped every month in the Shiva temple in Thrissur. He used to go to this temple on the last day of the month and worship on that day and the next, so that he could fulfil his religious obligations for two months with just one visit. Years passed and the ruler became older and weaker but he was reluctant to stop visiting the temple in Thrissur.

On one of these visits he managed to have his bath on the last day of a month and, helped by his entourage, went to the presence of the deity in the temple. He prayed in despair, "Oh benevolent Lord, I cannot bear the prospect of stopping this practice but I am finding it difficult to make these visits. Please have mercy on me and let me come to sit at your feet." That night he dreamt that someone came to him and assured him that there was no need for him to visit Thrissur again to see the deity. "I shall be coming to Nakkara Hill," the visitor in the dream seemed to say, "I shall have a bull in front of me and a white flower behind." The ruler woke up but saw nobody. He knew his visitor was Shiva Himself and fell asleep again feeling more at ease.

On his way back from Thrissur the ruler decided to worship at the famous temple in Vaikom. There he came across a sad-looking man with long hair and beard wearing a necklace of rudraksha beads and sacred ashes on his body. On enquiry about the identity of this person the ruler was informed that this man was a local Nambudiri Brahmin

---

*Thirunakkara Devanum Avitathe Kaalayum

who was staying there praying for some relief from his intense poverty and some means with which to get his daughters married. The ruler summoned the Nambudiri and suggested that he accompany him in which case the latter would try to help him get at least one or two of the daughters married. The Nambudiri happily agreed and joined the ruler's entourage.

In those days the ruler of Thekkumkur lived in a place called Thaliyil, a mile north of the Thirunakkara temple. That was where the Nambudiri began to live with the ruler.

One day the Nambudiri took the ruler's permission to visit a saint who lived in Thirunakkara and seek his financial help. The saint requested the Nambudiri to spend the next few days there as they were religious holidays and agreed to offer whatever little help he could.

The present location of the Thirunakkara temple was a jungle in those days and was known as the Nakkara Hill. The servants of the saint grew various tubers on the hill and it was the practice for the saint to arrange a feast at the end of that religious period. As was usual at that time of the year the servants went to the hill to collect the tubers for the feast. At a particular spot, as they dug, the ground began to ooze blood. Frightened by this sight they ran to the saint and apprised him of what they saw. The saint hurried to the spot and on digging further came across a rock in the form of a *shivalinga* or a representation of the God Shiva. As the tradition demanded that immediate puja or ritual of worship be conducted and offerings made to such a find, the Nambudiri was given the task of fulfilling this requirement. The ruler was also promptly informed.

The ruler was delighted that his dream in Thrissur had come true and he visited Nakkara without delay. He then saw a bull-like rock formation in front of the rock idol and a white flower behind it. This confirmed the ruler's view that it was indeed the deity from Thrissur who had come to Nakkara to redeem his promise.

The ruler immediately arranged for a temple to be designed and built with four towers, prayer halls, and such facilities. All the necessary funds and land were allocated and rituals commenced. Three annual festivals were also planned. The Nambudiri was appointed the head priest, two local families were assigned the right to provide services connected with the rituals, and the families of selected servants of

114

the saint were given the privilege of carrying the lamps during temple processions and pounding of rice for the offerings to the deity. The temple thus flourished and became famous as Thirunakkara temple or the holy Nakkara temple.

Soon thereafter the local population was faced with a major problem. A white bull was seen breaking into the farms in that area and destroying or eating up the crops. Nobody knew where it came from or where it went. Neither could anybody catch the bull. On moonlit nights the bull could be seen clearly but it always managed to escape before anyone could get near it.

On one moonlit night a farmer saw the bull among his crops and pelted it with stones. The same night the ruler had a dream in which a bull went to him and complained, "You have made all arrangements for my Lord but why have you not done anything for me, the Lord's means of transport? I am reduced to stealing my food from lands belonging to others and being pelted with stones. This is indeed a sad state to be in." Astrologers were summoned to interpret this dream and they confirmed that this was indeed the deity's bull. Arrangements were immediately made for offerings of food to be made to the idol of the bull and for these offerings to come from that very land where the bull was pelted with stones. That land is even today known as "Kaala Kandam" or the "land of the bull". So it happened that for the rest of his days the ruler was able to make his monthly visits to Thirunakkara temple instead of Thrissur.

The fame and name of the Thirunakkara temple spread and it was deluged with offerings and requests for many rituals. Very soon the Nambudiri was unable to cope with the work as head priest and had to enlist the services of another Nambudiri to assist him. The head priest ceased to be poor and eventually decided to return to Vaikom leaving the rituals in the hands of his assistant. However, a member of the head priest's family used to visit the temple once a month for many years to conduct the rituals.

It so happened once that one of the men from a family which provided services for the rituals fell foul of the ruler who ordered him to be shot. Unfortunately the soldiers mistook the priest for the offender and shot him dead. The priest's wife committed suicide at the entrance to the temple. It was ordered then and there that the community of the families that helped with the rituals would no longer perform those duties. It was also decided by the ruler that Nambudiri ladies would not be allowed inside the temple. Both these bans exist to this day.

The Lake Temple*

The story of a unique herbal remedy with which a temple first cured mental ailments and thereafter even major illnesses such as leprosy and cancer.

Thiruvizha temple is located in Cherthala taluk in the erstwhile Travancore State, now in Kerala.

The land on which the temple stands belonged once upon a time to the well-known family of Arakkal Panikkar. It was a jungle and had a lake in it. Around the lake lived a tribe of hunters whose main food was tortoises fished out from the lake. The hunters probed the bed of the lake with long poles which forced the tortoises to the surface where it was easy to catch them. One day a tribal woman was probing for tortoises when her pole struck something hard and blood was seen rising to the surface of the lake. Stricken with fear she raced to the owner of the land and gave him the news. He in turn informed other local dignitaries who went to the lake which by then had turned completely red. All of them together tried to bale out the water from the lake but discovered that days and nights of effort made only enough difference to the level of the water to reveal the top of what appeared to be a stone idol. It was obvious that the blood was flowing from this idol.

At this point of time a saintly-looking person appeared on the scene and said, "This is the idol of lord Mahadeva (or Shiva) and you will never be able to either bale out all the water or see the base of the idol. If you fill up the lake, build a temple, and commence worship of the idol there will be prosperity in this area. Meanwhile I shall stop the flow of blood." He then took some sacred ashes from his bag and using the pole put some on the idol. This immediately stopped the bleeding and the saintly person vanished leading to the belief that he was none other than Lord Mahadeva Himself.

---

*Thiruvizha Mahaadevanum Avitathe Marunnum

The people set about collecting money to fill up the lake and build the temple. Only the top of the idol was visible in the end but all rituals commenced in the temple. Even today the idol is submerged during the rainy season and the rituals are conducted from the banks of the lake. The temple prospered thanks to offerings and good management.

Not far from the Mahadeva temple there was a Vishnu temple which was ransacked during a Muslim conquest. The Nambudiri families which looked after the affairs of this temple fled but they were given the responsibility of managing the affairs of the Mahadeva temple also. This they did by frequent visits and these are documented until the Malayalam year 1052 (corresponding to 1877 of the modern calendar) after which the family of Chethuveli Marars seems to have taken over.

The temple became known for its power to cure mental illnesses. It so happened that a violently mad man began to frequent the temple. The Thalakkat Nair family was responsible for carrying out the menial work in the temple and depended on the temple for its livelihood. Unable to bear the torment of the mad visitor one of the Nairs prayed to Lord Mahadeva for help. That night a man appeared in a dream and said to the Nair, "Fear not. Do as I say and you will be safe. When the mad man comes tomorrow evening tie him up in front of the temple. The morning after that you will find a special green herb in the temple yard. Give it to the priests to crush and mix with milk. This is to be placed near the deity during the ritual of worship. Three coins are also to be placed and the mad man is to be given the medicine. In a short time from then he will bring it all out. Then he is to be fed the *payasam* (a traditional pudding) offering from the temple. He will regain his sanity after which he should be free to go." The Nair acted accordingly, the mad man was cured and the Nair was free to go about his work.

The fame of this medicine spread fast and people came from far and near to benefit from it. Those who came to the temple were not only Malayalis but also from other parts of the country and various castes. The management increased the temple rates all round but this did not deter people from coming. On the other hand the numbers continued to increase. Patients brought to the temple in shackles went away free and totally cured. Temple records show that even a prince of the

119

Travancore royal family was cured of his ailment in 1068 Malayalam Era (1893 according to the modern calendar).

In course of time the remedy was being used with good effect to cure major illnesses such as leprosy, cancer, and so on. Those who were subjected to black magic through poisoning would bring out the poisonous substances which had stayed undigested for days. Those influenced by evil spirits would also go into a trance in the presence of the deity after the afternoon rituals in the sanctum sanctorum and be released from the evil influence.

It will be recalled that the local people had already collected funds for the temple when it was built and set up a management to run its affairs. With the gathering popularity of the medicinal herb the earnings of the temple increased. In addition, the Travancore government also gave it financial support. With increasing wealth the rituals of the temple became wider in their range and periodic festivals were also added. Musical accompaniments traditional to temples such as percussion and other instruments were introduced in greater variety.

The medicinal herb used in the Thiruvizha temple is unique to that area. The name of the herb is not known to anyone. The herb itself assumes different colours once it is plucked, changing from green to blue, then red, black, yellow, and finally white. The medicine has to be prepared by the priests but the responsibility for plucking the herb continues to rest with the same Thalakkat Nair family.

As mentioned earlier a Vishnu temple nearby was ransacked by invading Muslim forces. The idol itself was removed and was missing for years. It was then established that the idol had been thrown into the temple pond. The local people built a new temple but the idol has not yet been re-established. It is hoped that when this is done Lord Vishnu would add to the prosperity of the place.

Thripunithura Festivals*

*The strong relationship between God and His devotees
is illustrated in the two following anecdotes.*

Thripunithura temple in Kochi (formerly Cochin, now in Kerala State) has three festivals and they are in the Malayalam months of *Chingam* (August/September), Vrischikam (October/November), and *Kumbham* (February/March). The Vrischikam festival is the oldest and the most spectacular and is the one dedicated fully to the deity "Thripunithura Appan".

The Chingam festival is known as the *Mooshari Ulsavam* or "Artisan's" festival and has the following origin. The idol of the deity was damaged and had to be replaced. A *mooshari* or artisan who was also a great devotee was summoned to cast another idol out of the traditional *panchaloha* or a combination of five metals – gold, silver, iron, copper, and brass. The metals were melted but despite several attempts the molten metals refused to mix correctly. The frustrated artisan cried out to the deity Thripunithura Appan in despair, "Oh my Lord Thripunithura Appa, please let the metals mix." It is said that the metals mixed to form the idol and in the process the devoted artisan also merged with the idol.

The Kumbham festival is attributed to a young maiden who was born in a Nambudiri family. Being the first born the baby was treated with more than ordinary parental love. Baby girls were often looked upon with some disfavour perhaps because of the additional burden of getting them married. The astrologers had forecast bad times for the girl in her first twelve years and so her parents were advised to make sure that she prayed in the Thripunithura temple every day. This advice was

---

*Thripunithura Kshetrathile Utsavangal

followed scrupulously and after she grew up she continued to visit the temple willingly and happily. In fact she did not even sip water until after she had prayed to Thripunithura Appan.

Then came the time when a young Nambudiri from a rich and aristocratic family expressed his desire to marry the young woman. Astrologers confirmed this as a good match and the marriage was fixed. The young woman was in distress over this decision, not because the marriage would take her away from her parents to the far off residence of her husband but because she would not be able to see her Thripunithura Appan every day. On the eve of the marriage she went to pray to her beloved deity. "My Thripunithura Appa," she cried, "I shall be married tomorrow morning and then I shall have to go away from here. I shall not be able to come here and pray to you every day. It is better for me to die than to give up my visit to the temple. My Lord, find me a way out of this." It is said that Thripunithura Appan drew her into the sanctum sanctorum and held her in an embrace after which she merged with the idol. Her bangles, rings and other ornaments were found lying at the feet of the idol. The festival in the month of Kumbham is dedicated to this young woman and during this festival Thripunithura Appan makes a visit to her family home. This visit is marked by much rejoicing in the Nambudiri home as Thripunithura Appan is received with a feast and presented with a ring. Thripunithura Appan gives the inmates of the home the traditional gifts of cloth. These practices are maintained to this day and one has to assume that the story of their origin is true.

A Voice Muted by Pride*

*How ambition leads to hard work, hard work to success,
and success, often, to arrogance ending with disaster.
This is the story of a renowned exponent of the ancient
performing art of koothu in Kerala.*

Long ago there was a very learned man named Ambalapuzha Sankaranarayana Chakyar who happened to go to Thiruvananthapuram (erstwhile Trivandrum) in the Malayalam year 1022 (1847 in our modern calendar). With the assistance of the ruler of the Kilimanoor principality he was given an audience by the Maharaja of Travancore and the opportunity to conduct a twelve-day koothu in the local Thiruvambadi temple.

The Maharaja attended the koothu just once after which he was not seen. This upset Chakyar who asked his sponsor, the Kilimanoor ruler, why the Maharaja was not patronising the koothu with his presence. This message was relayed to the Maharaja who commented, "Chakyar was explaining the meaning of the verses very well but the language lacked sweetness." At the end of the twelve days Chakyar was given only his fee for the koothu but not the customary gifts. Disappointed but not discouraged by this treatment Chakyar resolved that he would return and conduct another koothu to the Maharaja's satisfaction. He left for Kanyakumari (formerly Cape Comorin) where he worshipped in the local temple for a year. Again with the help of the Kilimanoor ruler he sought and received from the Maharaja another koothu assignment in the same temple in Thiruvananthapuram. Four or five days passed with no sign of the Maharaja attending it. The Kilimanoor ruler's enquiry revealed that the Maharaja did not wish to see the same kind of performance that he had seen once. The Maharaja was assured that Chakyar had improved his performance considerably. From the next day the Maharaja was present at the koothu and was very impressed.

---

*Ambalapuzha Sankaranarayana Chakyar

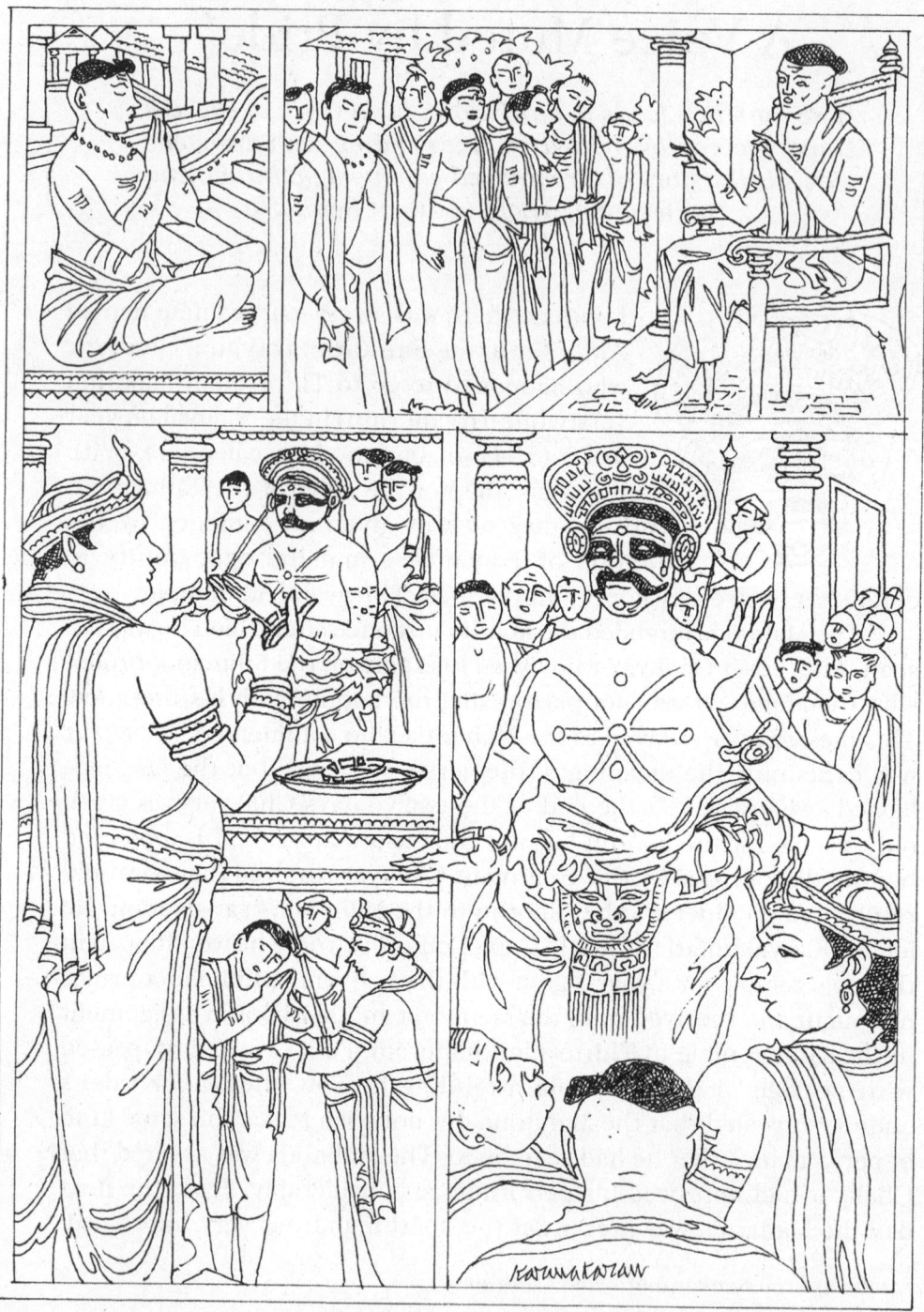

He rewarded Chakyar lavishly at the end of the twelve days and sent him on his way.

Chakyar's fame spread far and wide and it was acknowledged that his koothu performances were unsurpassed in the clarity of his explanations and the sweetness of the language. Unfortunately Chakyar gradually became afflicted with the undesirable consequences of success – arrogance, contempt for his peers, greed, and so on. He rejected requests for performances from all except rulers and the rich and the famous. At this time a group of eminent priests, scholars in scriptures and others was passing through Ambalapuzha where Chakyar lived and they made persistent requests for a special koothu as they had only heard about it. Chakyar declined the request although they said that they had planned to stay that night on the assumption that Chakyar would heed their request. Chakyar was unmoved despite offers of monetary reward. When the visitors continued to plead with Chakyar he was quite angry and curtly dismissed them saying they could ascertain his convenience on their way back.

The visitors who were all part of the elite of the local academic and spiritual community were very disappointed as their requests had always been respected and never spurned. They had in this case departed from their usual tradition of conveying their requests through messengers and had instead called on Chakyar themselves with their request. Overcome by the humiliation and much anger the seniormost of them, a highly renowned scholar, asked Chakyar one more time whether he would relent. Chakyar would not. The scholar then asked, "What if you are unable to speak when we come back?" Chakyar was about to respond when he found he could not speak. He remained in that state, filled with remorse, long after the visitors left until he came to the end of his days.

A Voice Muted by Pride

The Kottarakara Cow Shelter*

A Nambudiri destined to die young is saved by divine power and shows his gratitude by building a shelter for cows considered to be sacred animals.

In Kottarakara in Kollam division there is a Shiva temple managed by the local ruler. The royal family looked upon Lord Shiva as their family deity. However, when Kottarakara became part of Travancore State, the temple was also taken over by the Travancore government. On the southern side in the temple property there still stands a cow shelter and this story narrates its origin.

In British Malabar there lived a Nambudiri family which had no children. Years of rituals, worship, and acts of charity finally gave them a son and, naturally, great joy. However, this joy was shortlived as the baby's horoscope showed that he would die of snakebite at the age of twenty. The parents were so distraught that they even wished the baby had not been born. The baby grew into a bright and handsome lad and he was educated in all the subjects that a Brahmin needed to be. Very soon he became a scholarly young man but the parents remained sad at the son's inevitable fate. When the young man came to know about his parents' anxiety and its cause he reassured his parents saying he would seek the protection of the same Lord Shiva who is believed to have saved the sixteen-year old Markandeya from Yama, the Lord of Death.

The young man left his home and went on a pilgrimage to all the temples in the neighbourhood, finally reaching Aranmula. He spent forty-one days worshipping the deity there and on the final night he had a vision. The vision reminded him that he was then twenty years of age and advised him to go to Kottarakara to worship in the temple there. He believed that the vision was none other than the Aranmula deity and left for Kottarakara the following day.

*Kottarakara Goshaala

He commenced worship in the Kottarakara temple and one evening he went to the temple pond for a bath There suddenly he saw a serpent moving towards him and he realised this was the threat predicted in the horoscope. He placed his full faith in the temple deity and went about his evening rituals in the pond. The serpent waited ashore. After the ablutions the young Nambudiri slipped out of the pond on the other side and headed for the temple. The serpent pursued him there and the young man dashed towards the sanctum sanctorum where he prostrated. The sanctum sanctorum was closed for a ritual and the serpent attacked him. However, before it could bite, a kite flew in, picked up the serpent and flew away. It was reported later that the dead serpent was dropped outside the temple by the kite. The young man knew that the threat of snakebite had passed and he left for home the next day.

After a few days the Nambudiri was back in Kottarakara with some money. He took the ruler's permission to renovate the temple and to its south he also built a shelter for cattle. This shelter was built entirely in granite and is visible even today. He also built a shrine where the serpent fell and this shrine also exists and draws worshippers to this day.

A Brahmin in
Muslim Disguise*

*How a Brahmin youth infiltrated the Muslim community
to acquire skills in indigenous medicine and how he was
excommunicated by his own community on flimsy grounds
but left behind a treasure trove of knowledge.*

There was a time long ago when, thanks to the Muslim invasion, all the scriptures and documents relating to medical skills were in the possession of Muslims. This resulted in the disappearance of Brahmin teachers and scholars in the field of medicine. On the other hand the Muslim community could boast of many medical practitioners of repute. The Brahmins conferred on how to retrieve their lost skills. They knew they could not recover the scriptures by force. Neither could they offer to be students of the Muslim practitioners as they would not be accepted. The only option seemed to be for one of them to pose as a Muslim and seek training with a renowned Muslim practitioner. It was decided that one of the young and bright Brahmins, twenty-year-old Vakbhatacharian, would be the best choice as he was well-versed in the Hindu scriptures and history. Vakbhatacharian agreed to go disguised as a Muslim and become the student of a famous Muslim doctor who worked across the river from where the Brahmins had held their conference. He accordingly arranged for clothes and other material for his disguise and on a suitable day completed his morning rituals as a Brahmin, changed into his Muslim disguise and called on the Muslim doctor.

The doctor questioned Vakbhatacharian in detail about his antecedents and said he would have to be tested before being accepted. Vakbhatacharian answered the doctor in such a way that there was no cause for suspicion. He also did brilliantly in the tests and was asked

---

*Vakbhatacharian

to join the many other disciples already being trained. He was invited to stay in the doctor's residence where all his expenses would be taken care of. However, Vakbhatacharian explained to his teacher that he preferred to stay across the river with his relations and attend his classes from morning to evening.

Vakbhatacharian performed his morning worship and other rituals every day and went to his classes. Late in the evening he was back at home in time for his evening rituals after which he had his dinner and went to bed. The teacher and his student were both happy with each other and the former showed increasing enthusiasm in imparting his knowledge and skills to Vakbhatacharian. One evening the doctor suggested to Vakbhatacharian that it would be a good idea for him to continue his lessons at night so that there would be no interruptions or distractions on account of others. Vakbhatacharian readily agreed seeing this as an opportunity to complete his education as early as possible and reduce the risk of his real identity being discovered. So he returned to his teacher every night after dinner, worked through the night and returned home in time for his morning ablutions after which he was back in class on time. Thus the normal education ended but the teacher continued to impart greater and special skills to Vakbhatacharian.

One night in the middle of the lessons the teacher complained of a severe ache in his leg and asked Vakbhatacharian to massage his leg. Vakbhatacharian began to massage his teacher's leg when he fell into a near reverie. He bemoaned his plight, that of a true high-caste Brahmin well-versed in the holy scriptures having to sit massaging the leg of a low-caste. This and such other thoughts affected him so much that tears came into his eyes and these fell on the teacher's legs. The teacher who was lying with his eyes closed opened his eyes and seeing Vakbhatacharian's tear-laden eyes realised that he was not a Muslim but an impostor. Taking his sword the doctor went after Vakbhatacharian who fled for his life. At one point Vakbhatacharian had no option but to leap from the high building. Apart from a leg injury and a consequent limp he did not suffer any other harm. He fled back home and was asked by the other Brahmins how he managed to acquire a limp. He explained the reason and the next question was "What belief did you have on the strength of which you jumped from a high building?" Vakbhatacharian said, "I said to myself that if

131

there is truth in the assertion of the scriptures that God exists then no harm will befall me." The Brahmins thereupon took exception to the doubt he had expressed in the existence of God and promptly excommunicated him.

Vakbhatacharian was sure that no other person would be able to infiltrate the Muslim community as he had done. He spent the next few years ensuring that the result of his years of labour was not lost. He wrote *Ashtangasangraha* which was the summary of the medical sciences in prose and verse. Not satisfied with this he wrote *Ashtangahridaya*, another summary but with greater clarity and content in verse which could be committed to one's memory with more ease than the *Sangraha*.

He followed this up with *Amarakosha* written for general use on the lines of a lexicon and a summary of other similar writings.

Vakbhatacharian submitted these writings to the Brahmin community and disappeared never to be heard of again. The Brahmins were not too sure whether they should accept the writings of a person excommunicated but practical sense prevailed and the writings were formally accepted. However, as a reminder of the devalued status of the author it was decided that the three books written by Vakbhatacharian should not be read on the auspicious Ekadashi days, a practice followed to this day.

The Power of Faith*

A funny story with a lesson at the end – that strong belief and devotion are superior to mere knowledge and a presumption of one's own wisdom.

There was once a famous *visha vaidyan* (practitioner of anti-venom treatment) who was trained by the even more renowned Karat Nambudiri. He would not visit any patient but patients approached him in large numbers, got treated, and went back happy. He made no demand for any fee but the patients rewarded him well and he became quite wealthy.

In the same town near the vaidyan's house lived a lad named Kochuraman. His family was very poor and barely managed to survive. Kochuraman was in despair about his difficult circumstances and decided to learn to treat venom cases. Unfortunately he was illiterate and not bright at all. He asked those around him how to set about learning this new skill. He was told to approach a practitioner of this skill, offer him a fee that he could afford and then learn a mantra or magic verse which had to be repeated with devotion as many hundred thousand times as it had letters. Thereafter he could cure venom cases by applying to the injured spot, water or sacred ashes over which the mantra had been recited. Reassured by this advice he decided to approach the famous practitioner who lived nearby.

As Kochuraman had no money he decided to make an offering in kind and for this he picked a few gourds from the garden. He then presented himself at his neighbour's doorstep before dawn one day. When the practitioner woke up and opened his front door he saw Kochuraman there with his load of gourds. Kochuraman humbly made his request to which the vaidyan responded angrily *"Viddhi! Kushmandam endina?"* meaning "Fool! Why the *kushmandam* (gourds)?" In his anxiety and excitement Kochuraman heard only the words "Viddhi Kushmandam". He decided that the interview had ended

---
*Viddhi! Kushmandam

and the magic verse was "Viddhi Kushmandam". He promptly took leave of the vaidyan and returned home where he had a bath and sat down to repeat the mantra "Viddhi Kushmandam" as many hundred thousand times as the verse had letters!

While experts in treating venom cases never visited patients Kochuraman would happily go to where the patient was. The new practice became very popular and Kochuraman was not only kept busy but also became known for his consistent success. Thus he soon became a wealthy man.

It so happened that the then ruler of Kozhikode needed urgent treatment against venom. Many experts tried to cure him but failed and the ruler's family prepared for the last rites. It was at that stage that someone present suggested that Kochuraman be summoned for a last effort to revive the ruler. After much detailed discussion and despite some dissent it was decided to call Kochuraman.

He arrived soon and examined the patient. He then called the chief cook and asked him to make some rice gruel immediately. "His Highness has not had any food for three days and he will need it when he wakes up," was Kochuraman's explanation to a gathering which heard this in total disbelief. Kochuraman then took some water and recited the sacred verse over it and sprinkled it on the ruler who promptly opened his eyes. He did this twice more and the ruler sat up and complained of hunger. The gruel arrived and when the ruler was feeling much better he met Kochuraman whom he rewarded lavishly. The other experts including Kochuraman's guru or teacher were filled with surprise and shame. The guru assumed that when he was spurned Kochuraman must have gone elsewhere and acquired his skill.

The ruler ordered that Kochuraman be sent home ceremonially in a palanquin to the accompaniment of music and with suitable escort.

As Kochuraman was on his way he turned round and saw his guru among the crowd. He immediately alighted from the palanquin and rushing to his guru, prostrated before him and placed all the gifts at his feet. He thanked the guru for his mantra and apologized profusely for not visiting him earlier. The guru was intrigued and told Kochuraman that he had not passed on

135

The Power of Faith

any mantra. In fact he said he would be happy to learn from Kochuraman the mantra used to revive the ruler. Kochuraman assured his guru he had only one mantra and that was the one taught by the guru. One can well imagine the consternation on the guru's face when he was informed that the mantra which was so effective thanks to hundreds of thousands of times of dedicated repitition was "Viddhi Kushmandam"!

The Origin of A Great Poet*

A good deed is rewarded with a blessing and a baby boy is born who becomes a great poet.

A very poor Nambudiri from Vanneri was unable to get his daughters married and decided to travel to seek financial help from outside. He met rulers, the nobility and others from various parts of Malabar, Cochin, and Travancore and was on his way home with the collection he had made. It was afternoon when he reached a village, hot and tired. He went to the local temple and called out to ask if the midday rituals were over. The priest said they were but he could still have a meal if he returned after a quick bath. The Nambudiri went to the temple pond, put aside the bag containing the money and had a quick dip in the pond. When he was ready to leave, he found the bag missing. Needless to say he was in great distress and he lost not only his appetite for food but also his very interest in life. He searched in vain and finally decided to return to the temple. His enquiries there revealed that nobody from the temple had gone to the temple pond at that time. He could hardly eat but he finished his lunch and rested awhile in the temple. He then began his weary journey home.

Months passed and the Nambudiri decided to set out again on his journey as before. He passed through many places before reaching the same village where he had rested in the past. It was evening and after a bath he went to the temple where the same priest recognised him. They had dinner together after which the Nambudiri raised the subject of his overnight stay. The priest invited him home where he was welcomed by the priest's wife with great cordiality. They then soon began to exchange stories about themselves and the families. The Nambudiri spoke of his daughters and his problems in getting them married. The priest complained that his wife's family was short of males and how they longed to have a son. In the course of this conversation the Nambudiri mentioned his previous visit when he had lost his bag with the money

---

*Kunjan Nambiar

he had collected. The priest's wife wished to know more about the lost bag and then disappeared inside the house. When she returned she had a bag with her which she handed to the Nambudiri. It was the bag he had lost and when he checked the contents he found all the money intact. The wife explained that a long time ago she had gone to the pond and found some cowdung lying on the steps. She picked this up to take back home and under this dung she found the bag which she had cleaned and stored. It was obvious that while the Nambudiri was bathing a cow had dropped its dung on the bag. The Nambudiri had searched all around and left disappointed.

The Nambudiri took out half the money in the bag and offered it to the priest's wife who was incensed. She refused to touch it saying that it was her obligation to return lost property to its rightful owner. She wished to have nothing but the Nambudiri's blessing. The Nambudiri promptly rose and placing both his hands on her head blessed her saying "May you have a brilliant son." Not much later the priest's wife conceived and to them was born a baby boy who in course of time became the famed poet Kunjan Nambiar.

Gopalan, the Chosen One*

*This is the story of how the famous elephant Gopalan
came to be owned by the Nambudiri family, Aavanaamanakkal,
which lived in Katalassery village in Thrishivaperur taluk
in Cochin State.*

Gopalan was an elephant with extraordinary intelligence and devotion. It is the custom in the temples of Kerala to gather as many elephants as they can afford to participate in the various festivals. These elephants are an impressive sight lined up in their gold plated head-dress, men holding tall, multi-coloured silken umbrellas atop the elephants and the tallest elephant carrying the deity. Wealthy temples own elephants whereas the less wealthy ones hire them from other temples or individual owners. All the elephants have their distinctive personalities and some of them acquire fame for their special characteristics such as stature, composure in the presence of massive and noisy crowds and facing loud and fiery fireworks and even their ability to restrain the less disciplined elephants.

Narayanan Nambudiripad of Aavanaamanakkal who lived till the year 1068 in the Malayalam era (corresponding to 1883) and is even now remembered for his qualities of truthfulness, kindness, fairness, and concern for others had long wished to own a tusker. He came to know that another well-known Nambudiri family, Paambumekkat, had a young tusker for sale. He set out to see this elephant accompanied by Krishnan Nair, an expert in reading and identifying the various characteristics of an elephant. The head of the Paambumekkat family confirmed that they had a young tusker for sale but confessed that the reason for the sale was that the young animal had a dark line on its tongue which was a bad sign.

---

*Aaavanaamanakkal Gopalan

Narayanan Nambudiripad and Krishnan Nair then went to see the elephant. Krishnan Nair examined the elephant and gave his verdict. "It is true that the dark line on the tongue is an inauspicious sign but the elephant has numerous other propitious indications which can only augur well for the owner." They went back to the owner who said, "If it had not been for the dark line on its tongue I would have got not less than five thousand rupees and I would still not have sold the young elephant for even ten thousand rupees. However, I am not likely to get five thousand rupees and you may have it for a thousand rupees." Overjoyed at this bargain, Narayanan Nambudiripad immediately paid the amount and brought the elephant over to his home with the help of a mahout. Thus did Gopalan come to Aavanaamanakkal family. He was only twenty years old but in size and majesty looked years beyond the twenty. His tusks, the size, and shape of his head, his bearing made him out to be an exceptional tusker.

When Gopalan was taken to Deshamangalam family, closely related to Avanaamanakkal, the head of that family was greatly impressed with the appearance of the elephant and its reasonable price. He suggested that Gopalan be the property of the joint family and promptly paid up the thousand rupees.

Gopalan displayed outstanding intelligence and as he grew in years his various other qualities also became more visible. He was never chained except during musth and he would without prompting occupy the space allotted to him in the property of the family. He was fed meticulously on time and even when his food was delayed he did not feed off the many coconut and banana trees that were in plenty around him. The children of the family used to play with him, hanging on to his tusks and tail but he was always gentle with them and even seemed to enjoy it.

After the morning ritual of worship in the family every day Gopalan would be waiting at the northern door of the kitchen to receive his share of sweetmeats, jaggery, banana, and coconut offered to the gods in the ritual. The matriarch of the family used to place all these in his mouth addressing him from time to time as "My son, my son," to which Gopalan would respond with a rumble indicating great happiness and contentment. These expressions of mutual affection would give the

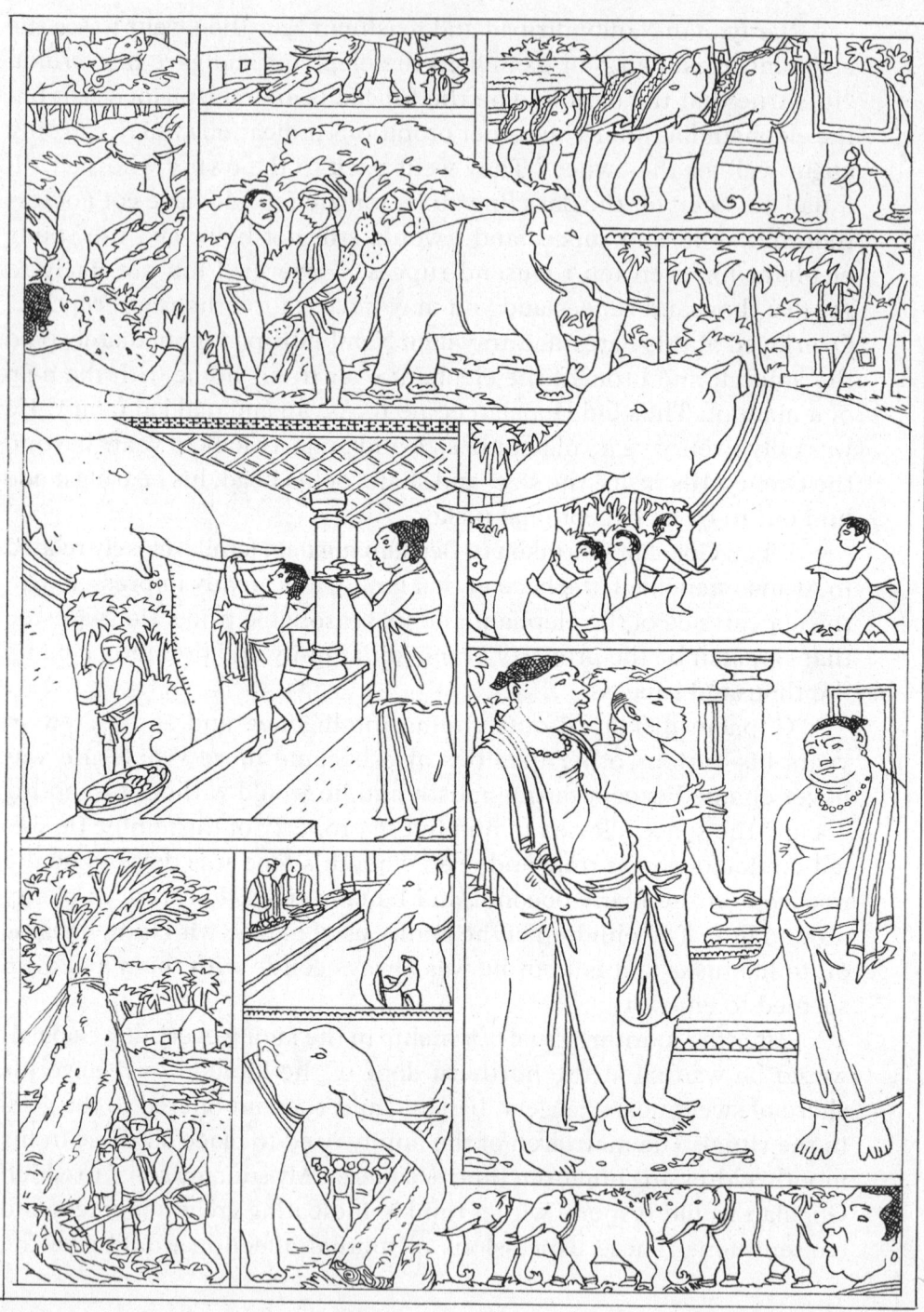

impression that the matriarch and Gopalan must have been mother and son in their last birth. Such was their genuine love for each other.

One day Gopalan presented himself at the kitchen door as usual for his share of the offerings. The matriarch placed rice and jaggery in Gopalan's mouth and went inside to fetch the other items. Just then one of the young children ran out and swung on Gopalan's tusks. Gopalan realised that if he closed his mouth the child would slide off the tusks and hurt himself. When the old lady returned she found Gopalan, mouth wide open with the youngster hanging on his tusks. The food had all slid out of Gopalan's mouth! Gopalan's gentleness caused great happiness all round.

There was a huge banyan tree to the south of the family home near a broken down well. It was decided to cut it down before it fell and caused damage around it. A large number of men tied ropes round the trunk and held on while it was being cut so that it did not fall into or on the well. Unfortunately when it was cut it fell into the well. In order to retrieve the valuable tree trunk the mahouts used Gopalan many times in vain. The head of the family then offered worship in their temple with special offerings of sweet *appams*, bananas, coconuts, jaggery and then lined them up in the front room outside which Gopalan would visit him every day. Gopalan was there as usual but seemed to take no notice of the lovely food displayed. The patriarch of the family addressed him, "Gopala, how can we just leave that tree trunk there? With you here it would be a shame not to move it from there. Please see if you can do something." Gopalan promptly turned round and first went round the broken down well as if to test the safety of its edge. He then knelt and with his trunk lifted the log upright and then slowly pulled it out of the well. As a final flourish he then flung the log to a side with a casual air! He then went back to enjoy all the food which he did not accept first as a bribe before performing the task but received it only as a reward for completing it.

Narayanan Nambudiripad was a devotee of Oorakathamma or the deity of Oorakam and he used to send Gopalan every year to carry the idol of this deity to the famous Aaratupuzha festival. Twenty-nine elephants line up for this festival and it so happened in one year that only twenty-six elephants were available. So Narayanan Nambudiripad arranged for three more elephants and these were chained beside

143

Gopalan, the Chosen One

Gopalan after the festivities concluded. Among these was one young elephant who ate up all his food and pulled a coconut-tree frond from Gopalan. Gopalan at once tossed three more fronds towards the young elephant. Not satisfied with this the young tusker attacked Gopalan who avoided the attack by stepping aside and dealt the attacker a hard slap with his trunk. The young elephant fell to the ground upon which all the mahouts came racing in and rescued the young animal. It was clear that Gopalan would not brook bad behaviour.

It was the custom that after the Aaratupuzha festival Gopalan would be given a bath and led to his parking place two miles away, carrying his feed of fifty palm fronds. On the way they had to pass through a narrow lane. As they were passing through this lane on one occasion a blind man was feeling his way forward in the opposite direction. The mahout was dozing atop the elephant and Gopalan himself did not have a clear view ahead because he was carrying the fronds upright to avoid the fence on either side. Suddenly the blind man heard the sound of the chains of the elephant and cried out in total fright. Gopalan was immediately alerted. He stopped and stepped backwards, dropped the fronds, lifted the blind man gently in his trunk and placed him carefully on the other side of the fence. He then picked up his load and went on his way.

On another occasion Gopalan was going to the river for a bath along a narrow lane when a low-caste pregnant woman came in the opposite direction. She saw the elephant and was in panic as she just could not get out of the way. Gopalan promptly stepped aside into a field to let the woman pass.

It was seldom that large elephants were equally good at carrying the deities at festivals and also working on logs. Gopalan was an exception. Having grown into a personable looking elephant Gopalan was chosen to lead all important processions in Cochin State. He had an impressive bearing which seemed to be enhanced every time he appeared in a procession decked out in all the temple finery.

Gopalan was the regular choice to carry the Paramaekkavu deity at the famous annual Thrissur *pooram* festival. As he walked from Paramaekkavu temple into the Vadakkunnathan temple he appeared to shrink in size to squeeze through the narrow eastern gate and out through the southern gate. However, once he joined the other elephants in the procession he seemed to have resumed his normal size and towered over them. When the drummers played their different rhythms Gopalan's ears flapped as if in recognition of these. He never attacked other elephants in a procession but did not brook any threat from them.

Gopalan was once carrying the deity of the Thripunithura temple at a procession and beside him was another elephant from Pazhur which happened to be in musth. As Gopalan did not like the smell of the musth he moved away to his left. The Pazhur elephant decided Gopalan would attack him and promptly attacked Gopalan. Gopalan stepped aside and turned to retaliate. The Pazhur elephant took fright and fled to a corner of the temple with Gopalan behind him. Gopalan gave him a gentle shove with his tusks causing only a minor injury to his attacker but pushing the Pazhur elephant's tusks into the wall. Thereafter Gopalan left to resume his position in the procession as if there had been no interruption.

All festivals are accompanied by commotion and noise but these did not disturb Gopalan in the slightest. At the Perumana festival six elephants were frightened by all the noise and broke their ranks. Gopalan stood his ground. Elephants have often run in panic frightened by the explosions in firework displays. Only during his musth did Gopalan show his dislike for fireworks but then human beings also show such dislike when they are not in the best of health.

During the Thrissur pooram festival, from the time Gopalan was decked out in the heavy gold and silk finery and the deity was placed on him, until the deity was taken back to the temple, Gopalan needed no guidance from the mahout. He knew when to walk and when and where to stop.

We have already said Gopalan was skilled in the work of moving logs, however big and heavy they were. Vellakkal Sankunny Menon, a prominent member of many temple managements and an organiser of the Thrissur pooram festival, had taken a timber lease in three hill sites in Cochin State. Gopalan was the chosen elephant during Menon's entire lifetime for his logging operations. It was also Menon who brought Gopalan into the pooram line-up in Paramaekkavu temple and ensured his regular participation.

While Gopalan was a willing worker with the logs he displayed his resentment at those who tied the tugging ropes on the logs with which the elephants moved the logs. It was almost as if Gopalan held those who tied the ropes responsible for his having to move the logs! Gopalan was, therefore, brought to the logs only after the ropes were tied.

Once a worker, Sankaran, was still tying the rope to a log on the Paravattani hill site when Gopalan appeared. Sankaran promptly hid himself. Gopalan had commenced his work when Sankaran, in moving back to a better hiding place, fell off the edge of the hill into the nearby river. He was struggling to save himself when Gopalan heard the commotion. He immediately put down the log and walked down to the edge of the river and extended his trunk towards Sankaran. Thus Sankaran was saved and Gopalan displayed presence of mind and no animosity at a time of crisis.

The Aavanamanakkal family had another elephant, Kuttikrishnan, who was as clever as Gopalan in logging work. However, Kuttikrishnan was mischievous and often deliberately dragged the logs to inaccessible places. It was soon decided that Kuttikrishnan would only work alongside Gopalan. With Gopalan by his side Kuttikrishnan was an obedient worker as he had a healthy respect for Gopalan's insistence on disciplined work. Even when Kuttikrishnan was in musth and in a threatening mood Gopalan's presence appeared to be able to calm him down.

Gopalan would never touch any food unless permitted by the mahout. One day the elephant was passing through a field belonging to the Deshamangalam family – an associate of the Aavanamanakkal family – when they came across a jackfruit tree laden with fruit. The mahout asked the person on the field if he would let Gopalan have a few of the jackfruits as the elephant and the field belonged to virtually the same family. The man answered rudely saying he had leased the property and his contract did not say he had to feed the elephant free. The mahout said nothing but as they were leaving he muttered angrily to himself, "I wish there isn't a single fruit on that tree tomorrow morning", Gopalan overheard this remark and knew it was not meant for him to hear. However, after midnight that night he walked softly away from where he usually spent the night and made straight for the field they had passed earlier in the day. He then went up to the jackfruit tree and stripped it of all the fruits. After feeding on as many as he wished to he carried back what was left and presented them to the other elephants. Thereafter never again was any request on behalf of the elephants spurned by anybody.

Gopalan was endowed with every good quality like intelligence, honesty, and discipline but he was guilty of one dreadful act. He drowned his mahout Atchutha Menon in the river where he had been taken for his bath but that was when he was in musth and barely conscious of what he was doing. When he finally realised what he had done he was filled with a terrible sense of guilt and remorse.

When Gopalan was living in Deshamangalam he was taken for his bath to the Deshamangalam river, a branch of the bigger river Bharathapuzha. When one side of Gopalan had been washed he would turn over without any instruction but only after he had decided that he had been washed well! After his bath was done he would not wait till his mahout finished his. Gopalan would walk straight back home, enjoy the food specially kept for him and go to his designated "parking" place. The mahout would return much later after his bath and, before retiring for the night, collect and leave Gopalan's supper by his side.

Then came the day when Gopalan returned as usual after his bath early in the evening and ate the food kept for him at home. He then went towards a heap of ashes in the compound, picked some ashes with his trunk and flung them into the air. He then lay down with his head towards the south and breathed his last. One can imagine the grief and dismay among those around over this unexpected event. There was hardly anyone who did not cry on hearing the news and such cries and wails rent the air. Rites connected with his death were conducted as prescribed and three hundred *paras* of rice were cooked and distributed. It must be mentioned that Gopalan had left behind in his account his earnings of a lakh rupees paid for his presence at temple festivals and his work at logging sites!

Gopalan, the Chosen One

An Ideal Wife*

*Two brothers test their wives to decide what
an ideal wife should be like.*

The famous Brahmin Vararuchi had twelve sons by a low-caste wife. This story is about two of them, Agnihotri and Paakkanar. All the sons together except one always observed their father's death anniversary in Agnihotri's house and on one of those occasions when they sat down to lunch Agnihotri's wife showed some reluctance to serve their food. When she was eventually persuaded she appeared behind her customary umbrella. When Paakkanar questioned the need for this umbrella Agnihotri explained that a true wife was not expected to look at another man. Paakkanar challenged this practice saying that the qualities of a true wife were not judged by the use of an umbrella. He suggested that his was the true wife. A debate followed and it was decided that they would both go to Paakkanar's house to test Paakkanar's theory.

On reaching Paakkanar's house he summoned his wife and asked how much paddy they had at home. She replied they had five measures. Paakkanar then asked her to take a half, pound it into rice, and cook the rice. She immediately proceeded to do as her husband had told her and in a while produced the cooked rice. Paakkanar then asked her to dump the cooked rice in the garbage which she did without question. She was then told to take the other half of the paddy and repeat the process. She again pounded the paddy and cooked the rice. Paakkanar had that also thrown out, and all this when there was no more paddy and his wife had not eaten that day.

Paakkanarute Bharyayute Paathivrathyam

The two then returned to Agnihotri's house where he asked his wife to take two and a half measures of paddy, pound it, and cook the rice. She asked why this had to be done when they had rice already pounded and ready. When Agnihotri insisted she complied but she made her unwillingness obvious. When Agnihotri asked her to throw the cooked rice out she was very agitated. "Are you mad?" she asked, "I have worked hard to pound the paddy and cook the rice and now you want me to throw it out. This is unreasonable." When Agnihotri asked her to repeat the process she was adamant. "There must be a limit to madness. I am not prepared to dance to your every tune." Saying this she promptly left the scene. Paakkanar explained to Agnihotri that a wife is expected to obey the husband implicitly, willingly, and without question.

It is possible that this theory will be contested by the modern generation. However, it is to be hoped that all will agree that wives should not refuse to do their husbands' bidding giving lame excuses and producing futile arguments. It is acknowledged that a wife has the right and the obligation to reason with and dissuade a husband who makes improper demands out of obstinacy or lack of understanding.

There is another legend about how Paakkanar showed Agnihotri the power of his wife's devotion. When they happened to go to Paakkanar's home one day the wife was drawing water from the well. Paakkanar called out to his wife when the vessel with the water was halfway up the well. The moment Paakkanar called, his wife let go the rope and ran towards him. Agnihotri saw the strange sight of the vessel staying halfway up the well instead of dropping back into it. Our sisters in Kerala would do well to make a note of these legends which can only help them be true wives.

Kozhikode Market*

This is a recollection of a legend about how Lakshmi, the goddess of prosperity, still waits in Kozhikode Market for her meeting with the Dewan.

It so happened once upon a time long ago that the Zamorin or ruler of Kozhikode (formerly Calicut) suffered from unbearable pain in his right shoulder. Medical practitioners, astrologers, and those with magical powers were all summoned and despite their best efforts not only did the pain not abate but on the other hand became more intense. It was at this time that a person who appeared to be highly intelligent and perceptive appeared on the scene and enquired of the ruler about the nature of his ailment. On receiving the information he assured the ruler that the problem could be dealt with by applying a wet towel to the painful shoulder. Such a simple remedy did not impress anybody but they tried the treatment as they did not wish to ignore any option. The pain disappeared instantly and the happy ruler rewarded the successful practitioner generously.

Very soon after this incident the news reached the loyal and devoted Dewan or Prime Minister who reacted with great fear and shock. "Oh my God, all is lost," he remarked as he rushed out as if in search of someone. He wandered around the town and finally reached the local market by dusk. There he saw a stunning-looking young woman whom he approached and addressed, "I have to tell you a very important secret." She asked him what it was and the Dewan suddenly looked harassed. He said, "I have just now remembered I have left my seal in the office and I have to go and fetch it. Please do not leave this spot till I return as what I have to say to you is extremely important."

---

*Kozhikode Angadi

Although she agreed to wait the Dewan was persistent. "Just agreeing to wait is not enough, please promise not to leave." The woman gave her word.

The Dewan returned to the ruler's presence and asked about his ailment. The ruler described the cure with great happiness. The Dewan then spoke. "If only Your Highness had known the cause of your ailment you would not have done what you did. It is too late to talk about all that. The prosperity we have enjoyed is because Goddess Lakshmi was residing in Your Highness. The pain was caused by the fact that the goddess was dancing on your right shoulder. Applying the wet towel was most inauspicious and forced Lakshmi to leave. The person who cured you knew this and deliberately recommended the treatment. Fortunately, although the goddess has left this spot I have managed to ensure that She does not leave Kozhikode." Saying this he left the ruler's presence and committed suicide. It should be clear by now that the beautiful woman in the market was none other than goddess Lakshmi who, it is believed, still stands in the market bound by Her promise not to leave until the Dewan returned. It is said that the market continues to flourish and that as dusk descends the market begins to take on a divine aura, take on a celestial glow.

The Spitting Habit*

This story illustrates the wisdom of using strong remedies for chronic ailments.

In the olden days the road leading from the western gate of the famous Padmanabhaswami temple to the Mitranandapuram temple was lined by the homes of the many Nambudiris who visited Thiruvananthapuram (formerly Trivandrum) to participate in the many religious rituals. These Nambudiris used to sit on the verandahs on both sides of the road, chew betel leaves, and spit into the road. This caused immense hardship to the devotees of the two temples but nobody complained out of the traditional respect for Nambudiris.

In the middle of the nineteenth century Marthanda Varma who was the heir to the Travancore throne was one day visiting the temples and had to go along the road connecting the temples. He found the road dirty and impassable because it was covered in betel-laden spit. He summoned the cleaners and had them clean the road after which he had both sides of the road lined with the sacred *tulsi* plant in the hope this would prevent the Nambudiris from spitting into the road.

Later the Maharaja Swati Thirunal visited the two temples and had to take the connecting road. There he found the tulsi plants lining the road but they were covered in spit. He enquired of his retainers who had planted the tulsi and was informed that the Elaya Raja or the heir apparent had planted tulsi to prevent spitting. The Maharaja laughed and said, "He is so innocent that he does not realize these methods do not work. We shall have to try something else." The Maharaja ordered all the tulsi plants to be removed. He posted a guard there displaying a set of handcuffs and the significance of this was not lost on the Nambudiris. There was not a drop of spit thereafter on the road!

---

*Randu Maharajakkanmarute Swabhaava Vithyasam

Loyalty is where Power is*

An illustration of how the loyalty of some is to power and not conditioned by personal regard.

One branch of the Vadakkumkur (a principality in erstwhile Travancore State) royal family at one time used to live in a place called Kaipuzha and the members of that arm were referred to as Kaipuzha Rajas. One of the Kaipuzha princesses was married to a prince from the Ambalapuzha (another principality) royal family. In a few years he built a palace in an area called Pulinkunnu and it was there that his wife and family lived. They continued to live there after the prince died as they had the right to collect local taxes and in any case they had been well provided for in terms of money and material comfort.

The Maharaja of Travancore went to war at this time against the ruler of Ambalapuzha and it was obvious that the latter would have to surrender. The princess was worried that Pulinkunnu would be attacked. She decided to move back to Kaipuzha and directed her staff to make all arrangements.

There were nearly three hundred wealthy Nair families in Pulinkunnu and a few Christian families which lived by doing menial work.

As the princess was virtually the ruler of Pulinkunnu all the local people owed allegiance to her and had great respect for her departed husband. However, when the Nairs heard that the princess was planning to leave Pulinkunnu their attitude changed. They did not even have the courtesy to call on her to offer their help. The servants summoned two boats into one of which they loaded all her possessions. The princess and her children entered the other boat but then discovered their staff had disappeared leaving them all alone in the boat. They waited for a long time but in vain and the princess was beginning to get desperate.

Kaipuzha Rajniyum Pulinkunnu Deshavum

Then they all began to cry. The princess sent her oldest son to seek help from the Nair families near by but he came back alone with the news that he had been ignored in every house. The young lad then went to the Christian families but found no one there. The sun was setting and the family was in a state of total helplessness.

A few Christians were walking along at a distance and the young prince was sent after them to try to get their help. When they saw their ruler they anxiously asked how she came to be in that situation. The princess explained to them why the family was leaving and offered them a generous reward in return for their assistance. The response of the Christians was not only favourable but it also reflected their loyalty to her. They refused any reward saying that it was their duty to help her. They requested the princess to let them have some time for a quick meal as they had been doing menial work all day. Very soon they were back and took over the two boats. The princess prayed for a safe journey. In her anger at the behaviour of the Nairs she cursed them saying that their wealth and status would decline. She prayed for the prosperity of the Christians.

The boats reached Kaipuzha at dawn the next day and the Christians and the servants there unloaded the boats. Famished after their experience the princess and her children had a hearty meal. The Christians were also fed and rewarded generously.

Soon after the princess's departure all of Ambalapuzha including Pulinkunnu fell to the army of the Maharaja of Travancore. The Nairs began to decline in status and numbers and soon not more than four or five families remained. The Christian families flourished in number and wealth. Astrologers later confirmed that the princess's curse and blessing had indeed been responsible for the reversal of fortunes of the two communities.

Devotion vs. Erudition*

*It is said that true devotion ensures divine grace.
The illustration of this truth is supported by the many writings of
the devotee concerned.*

Poonthaanathu Nambudiri, also known as Poonthaanam, was not considered well-versed in the Hindu scriptures. He was born in Angadippuram which was part of the old British Malabar which now forms part of North Kerala. He and the famous scholar Meppathur Bhattathiri lived during the same period in eighth century Malayalam Era or sixteenth century in the modern calendar.

After a long and anxious wait Poonthaanam had a son. At the ceremony held to feed the baby his first meal of rice, many Nambudiri families had gathered and the womenfolk placed their bundles of clothes in a corner of a room without realizing that the baby was sleeping in that corner. When the time came for the ceremony the mother found that the baby had died of suffocation. The trauma that afflicted Poonthaanam and his wife can be well imagined. Poonthaanam lost interest in everything and in his intense grief composed the famous *Gnanappaana*, the verses of which are recommended for reading by those suffering from deep grief. These verses are written in simple language which is clear in its meaning.

While in Guruvayur, Poonthaanam discovered that Meppathur Bhattathiri was also there composing his *Narayaneeyam*. Poonthaanam was composing the *Santhanagopalam* story in verse. Bhattathiri was conscious of his scholarship in Sanskrit and had looked down on Poonthaanam who was guileless and not as learned as he, Bhattathiri. Poonthaanam decided to request Bhattathiri to look through his composition of *Santhanagopalam* and suggest corrections. Bhattathiri's response was sarcastic. He said, "What is there to look at? It will be full of

---

*Poonthaanathu Nambudiri

mistakes as your knowledge of the language is doubtful." Humiliated by this reply Poonthaanam burst into tears in the presence of the deity. A voice then emanated from the sanctum santorum.

"Poonthaanam's *vibhakti* (scholarly Sanskrit) may not be as good as Bhattathiri's but his *bhakti* (devotion) is superior to Bhattathiri's." Much chastened by this Bhattathiri went to Poonthaanam and said, "You must forgive me for something I said without thinking. Your *Gnanappaana* is already well recognised and I shall be happy to look at your *Santhanagopalam*." Bhattathiri edited this composition and returned it with complimentary comments.

In the *Santhanagopalam* story Lord Krishna and Arjuna of the Pandavas go to Vaikuntam, the abode of the Gods, and Poonthaanam was worried that he could not describe Vaikuntam appropriately. It is said that Guruvayurappan, the deity of the Guruvayur temple appeared in

159

Devotion vs. Erudition

a dream and showed Poonthaanam what Vaikuntam looked like. It has been the custom in Guruvayur for the *Bhagavatham*, the story of Lord Krishna, to be read and explained by scholars. Devotees flocked to attend these sessions. Poonthaanam used to listen carefully and in course of time was able to explain the meaning of the verses. With his devotion to the Guruvayur deity his explanations were given with a lot of feeling and this appealed greatly to the audience. It was well known that Poonthaanam's explanations did not strictly adhere to the script of the *Bhagavatham*, but contained improvisations which added to the listener interest. Some of the scholars tended to get jealous of Poonthaanam's popularity. One such scholar got an opportunity – or so he thought – of embarrasisng Poonthaanam once when he was explaining the scene in which Rukmini was sending an emissary to her lover Krishna. Poonthaanam happened to say that Rukmini sent Krishna a letter, a point which was not in the script. The scholar immediately asked where in the script it was said

a letter was sent. This question did manage to halt Poonthaanam for a moment but then from the sanctum sanctorum came a voice which said, "Where is it said a letter was not sent? In fact I did receive a letter from Rukmini." This show of divine support silenced the scholar, pleased Poonthaanam, and amazed the audience.

People soon began to show great respect for Poonthaanam although he was not an acknowledged scholar in the formal sense. He was also given the first place in the dining room of the temple and very soon that place was considered to be his right. It so happened one day that a famous Nambudiri scholar was in Guruvayur temple and the temple manager decided that the visitor should have the first place in the dining room that day. Without being aware of this plan Poonthaanam occupied his usual place and was promptly asked by the manager to move. Poonthaanam was reluctant to do so and he was bodily removed from his seat. Poonthaanam could not bear this insult and walked out. He then heard this advice from the sanctum sanctorum, "Poonthaanam, you need not hereafter live among these wicked people or come here again. I shall come to your home whenever you wish to see me." Poonthaanam left Guruvayur and returned home.

Back in his residence Poonthaanam decided he would not touch his food till he had seen Guruvayurappan, the deity of the Guruvayur temple. The deity appeared before him on his left side and told him to stay at home and that Guruvayurappan's presence would always be with him. A small temple was built at that spot in which a Krishna idol was established and worship and rituals commenced. As Krishna appeared on the left side of Poonthaanam that temple came to be known as Idathupurathambalam or "left side temple". Having listened to *Bhagavatham* being read and explained for years, Poonthaanam soon began to compose verses in Sanskrit.

By Guruvayurappan's grace Poonthaanam had many children and lived for many years in this home with unwavering devotion to his Lord Krishna.

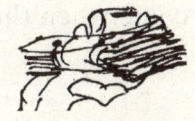

The Power of Illusion*

This narrative describes how Thamban's skills were tested and how the results far exceeded the expectation of those who demanded to see his display.

Few people have not heard of the skill achieved by Kaipuzha Thamban in medicine, sorcery, astrology, and magic in eleventh century Malayalam Era or the middle of the nineteenth century in the modern calendar. However, some of his exploits are being recounted here to ensure that they do not follow into obscurity those of many other similar great men before him.

Thamban was also called "Kunju" and "Kunju Thamban". He learnt his magic from that great magician Vattapparambil Valiathaan. Although his teacher was Valiathaan who had vanquished and driven out such renowned magicians as Peethambara Iyer and the Muslims who spread and sold their wares on the surface of the water, Thamban was like a torch lit from a wick, shining brighter than his teacher. However, he displayed most of his prowess only after his teacher's days.

Thamban was once in the presence of the then Maharaja of Travancore when the latter said Thamban had not visited him for a long time and that he should display some new tricks. Thamban was reluctant and said he had nothing new to show. The Maharaja was persistent and so Thamban agreed to think up of something to display when it was less warm. The Maharaja then asked him if he could use his astrological knowledge of planetary positions and predict the possibility of rain. Thamban's reply was prompt, "Let the planets be wherever they are. It will rain today." The Maharaja was surprised for he could see none of the usual signs that herald rain. Thamban then recited a verse which meant that the rains come when they wish to and neither gods

---

*Kaipuzha Thamban

nor humans know from where they come. The Maharaja was amused by this exchange and said sarcastically that maybe Thamban knew better than the gods.

As this conversation was concluding the skies turned dark. There was the crash of thunder and lightning flashed across the sky. It started to rain and very soon the river nearby began to rise. The water entered the compound of Shri Padmanabhaswami temple, the houses in the vicinity, and finally the verandah of the palace. The Maharaja was beginning to panic when a rowboat arrived and the oarsmen asked the Maharaja to board it without delay. As the Maharaja was about to step into the boat Thamban stopped him. In a moment the Maharaja realised that there was no rain, thunder, or lightning. The Maharaja confessed that Thamban's display was on the excessive side but wished to see another which would be for a wider audience.

The next day people flocked to the palace to witness Thamban's performance. Thamban did not disappoint them as he walked along the surface of the river, spread a blanket on the water, spread several articles on it and performed many astounding tricks. Thus Thamban's stay in Trivandrum ended and he went back home laden with gifts.

On another visit to the Maharaja, Thamban was persuaded to give yet another display. He spread a blanket in the palace yard and was about to commence his performance when a thread descended from the sky and to it was attached a letter. Thamban took the letter, read it and handed it to the Maharaja. It was a letter bearing the signature and seal of Indra, king of the Gods, saying that there was a fierce battle raging between the gods and the demons. Thamban's help was needed without delay. Thamban promised to continue his performance on his return and climbed up the thread, soon becoming invisible. Very soon blood started raining from the sky followed by severed limbs, then by corpses of soldiers and animals such as horses and elephants. In a short while Thamban's severed head dropped into the midst of the audience. The Maharaja's consort who was watching all this swooned and as the Maharaja was rising to go to her aid he heard Thamban's voice from behind, "There is nothing to worry about. Today's performance is over."

Thamban was once on a visit to the Panthalam ruler. The ruler said to Thamban, "It is a long time since you showed us some of your

tricks. It is late today and so we shall see them tomorrow." Thamban pleaded old age for his inability to perform but the ruler was adamant. Thamban said nothing and they retired for the night. They met next morning and were sitting on the bank of the river close by preparing for a bath when Thamban asked, "Do you have crocodiles here?" The ruler answered, "When the river is full we do see an occasional crocodile but never in this kind of summer." No sooner had he said this than a crocodile surfaced right in front of them. The ruler immediately rose while Thamban continued to sit there. The crocodile pounced on Thamban and carried him off into the river. Thamban screamed, "Your Highness said there are no crocodiles here and now you have fed me to one," as the crocodile pulled him beneath the surface. The ruler stood there struck dumb for a while and then summoned his servants and men with nets to make a thorough search for the crocodile and Thamban. Meanwhile crowds had also gathered on hearing the news. The search was futile and it was abandoned towards the afternoon. The ruler had his bath and went to the temple which was kept open for his daily visit. As he went inside the temple he saw Thamban sitting there immersed in prayer. He saw the ruler and asked, "What delayed Your Highness's bath today?" The ruler was unable to believe his eyes and said, "If I had known you were here I would not have been so late. You fooled me, didn't you?" Thamban answered, "Your Highness was insistent that I should show some trick today and wasn't that what I did?"

The above are examples of Thamban's prowess in magic. He was also a clever astrologer. He visited the Maharaja of Travancore who was insistent that Thamban should accurately predict the day and time of the Maharaja's death. Thamban was unwilling to do this as he said such a forecast would only create fear and confusion. The Maharaja persisted with his request and Thamban wrote out the exact date and time of the Maharaja's death. The Maharaja then asked Thamban when he himself would die. Thamban replied that he would die two years before the Maharaja.

As the day of Thamban's death approached the Maharaja sent his men with sandalwood logs, silk, and other requirements for his cremation to be stored secretly near Thamban's residence. The men were to stay there to hand over the material to Thamban's family if he died or bring it all back if he did not. When the predicted time arrived

Thamban asked his family to spread sand and grass on which he lay down and died reciting his prayer. The material and money sent for the cremation were handed over to the family and the ruler's men returned with the news that Thamban died exactly on the day and at the time forecast by him.

On hearing that Thamban's forecast was accurate in his own case the Maharaja began to panic and eventually lost his mind. He also died exactly as forecast by Thamban. Besides the stories narrated above there are also stories about Thamban's skills in medicine and sorcery but these will have wait till another occasion arises.

The Saint of Vilwamangalam*

This is the story of a saint who had the rare ability to see the gods and interact with them.

There cannot be many in Kerala who have not heard of Vilwamangalathu Swamiyar, the Saint of Vilwamangalam, who could actually see the gods. Thanks to this saint, many temples and events were established in Kerala.

Once on Karthika day in the month of Vrischikam in the Malayalam era the saint went to Vadakunnathan (Lord Shiva) temple in Thrissur but found the deity missing from the sanctum sanctorum. Wondering how he could worship an absent deity he circumambulated the temple and found the deity facing south and seated on the southern wall of the temple. He asked the deity why he was seated on the southern wall and the deity replied, "I am seated here to watch my love Karthiayani as she returns from her bath, all adorned and with much celebration." As in all temples which celebrate the ceremonial bath of the deity on the last day of the annual festival, Kumaranellur also has the same ritual but with the difference that the deity here, Goddess Karthiayani, has the ceremonial bath and procession every morning. This ritual is observed with even greater celebration on the ninth day, Karthika, of the festival. From that day every year on Karthika day in the month of Vrischikam, the Vadakunnathan temple in Thrissur has one puja or the ritual of worship at the southern wall of the temple.

On another occasion the Swamiyar (saint) visited the Vaikom temple on an *Ashtami* day and saw many Brahmins being fed. The deity was, however, missing from the sanctum sanctorum. The saint looked around and saw an old Brahmin seated near a pillar in the northern

*Vilwamanagalathu Swamiyar

dining hall of the temple. Although in disguise the deity was recognised by the saint and His presence announced to the others. Thereafter at every feast in the Vaikom temple a place was set for the deity near the same pillar. The Brahmins also began to consider it a privilege to participate in the feast in the northern dining room on Ashtami day.

The saint went to Ambalapuzha temple to worship during one of the festival days and found the deity missing. He soon found the deity disguised as a Brahmin serving food at the feast for the Marars or the drummers at the festival. The saint asked the deity why He was serving when there were enough men on this job. The deity replied, "These Marars work hard to make the festival in my temple successful and I have been coming here every year to see that they are looked after and fed well." Thus the annual Marars' feast assumed importance and it is assumed even to this day that the deity is present on this occasion.

There are many such stories about Vilwamangalathu Swamiyar. It is well known from local records that the temples in Thiruvanthapuram, Thiruvarpa, etc., were established thanks to the saint. It is believed that

168

the Cherthala Karthiayani temple was also thanks to his effort. The saint was once on his way along the road through Cherthala when in a forest area he saw seven damsels having their bath. It became obvious to the saint that these were not mere humans but celestial maidens and he went closer. The maidens ran away with the saint in pursuit. The damsels plunged into different lakes but the saint went in after them. Each of them was established by the saint in a different place. It so happened that the lake into which the seventh maiden jumped was full of mud. She resisted the saint's effort to take her ashore. He shouted at her, "You with mud on your head," which led to the place being called by its Malayalam translation Cherthala (*cheru* – mud, *thala* – head). Thus seven deities were established by the saint in Cherthala and the seventh was known as the Cherthala Bhagavathi or Cherthala goddess also known as Cherthala Karthiayani. Following the saint's abuse in his desperate effort to rescue her from the lake against her will, it has become the belief that She still likes to hear abusive songs sung at Her festival!

If all these many stories about the Saint of Vilwamangalam are true it raises the question whether this saint was only one person or different ones. If it was the one and only person one has to assume that his life span was much longer than that of a mere mortal. Many temples are attributed to the saint's effort and this cannot normally be over a period of a hundred years. However, it is also said that his contemporaries were many other saintly persons which would substantially increase the life span of Vilwamanagalathu Swamiyar.

The Priest of Katamattam*

A destitute lad becomes a priest who cures and has power over evil spirits.

Most of us in Kerala have heard of the Priest of Katamattam who was famous as a scholar of scriptures. He was born in a very poor family in Katamattam village in Kunnathunad taluk and was named "Poulose", a local version of "Paul". With the early death of his parents and with no siblings he was left alone in the world at a young age. With no means of livelihood Poulose's life in a little hut became unbearable. One day he left the hut and went to the local church where he prayed long and hard for an end to his suffering. As if by God's will the head priest of the church happened to visit the church at that time and see this young and pleasant lad in distress, engaged in fervent prayer. He called Poulose aside and asked him the cause of his agony and was apprised fully of the tragic circumstances of Poulose's life. The priest thereupon reassured Poulose and offered to look after him as he would his son with food, clothing, and shelter.

In a few days the priest found Poulose to be good-natured and bright and so arranged for his education with a good teacher. The priest himself taught Poulose the Syrian language and educated him in all that was necessary to make him a priest. In a few years Poulose became adept in Malayalam and Syrian languages and acquired the skills required by a priest. Soon, thereafter, Poulose was admitted to the first stage of priesthood.

The local priest had a large herd of cattle and a servant to look after them. This servant used to leave with the cattle early in the morning every day after a meal and carrying a packed lunch. The cattle were taken to the nearby hills to graze through the day and were brought back in the evening. One evening while they were returning the herd was attacked by a tiger which finally pounced on a cow. The herd

---
*Katamattathu Kathanar

scattered in fright while the tiger disappeared into the forest with its prey. The cowherd fled back screaming and reported the incident to the priest. So fond was the priest of his cows that he lost no time in getting Poulose and a few armed men and setting out for the forest. Having reached the forest the party split and the members dispersed in different directions in search of the herd. In a short while it was pitch dark and it was impossible to continue the search. The priest and his followers returned home by which time the entire herd barring the one carried away by the tiger had found its way back to the cowsheds. The priest was relieved that only one cow was lost and the others had returned safely.

That was when the priest discovered that Poulose was missing. He was filled with anxiety and grief which increased as time passed. He could neither eat nor sleep and kept walking restlessly up and down till dawn finally broke. He prayed hard to God and then headed for the forest accompanied by his followers to search for Poulose. Despite a thorough search they could find no trace of Poulose. When four or five days passed without any news of Poulose all except the priest were convinced that Poulose too had fallen prey to the tiger. The priest, however, was certain that God would not let any harm befall a good and devout Poulose and so continued to pray for his safety.

Poulose had not lost his life as assumed by all but he did run into some trouble. He had searched all over the forest for the cattle but did not find them. He was on his way back in disappointment. There is a belief that evil spirits occasionally lead wayfarers astray and it is possible that this was what happened to Poulose. He walked a great distance without realising that he had lost his way. After a long time he began to worry that he was no closer to home. It was so dark that he could not even retrace his steps and he could find nobody who could guide him. He stopped at the mouth of a huge cave.

As Poulose stood there lost in thought a man of frightful appearance pounced on him and carried him into the cave. The cave was dark as they entered it but soon lights appeared and Poulose was taken to a rather pleasant place. His captor then went up to a powerful looking man who was seated and whispered something to him. There were many who stood round this person in obvious awe. They were all without clothes and looked fearful but from the way all except one were standing it was obvious who the leader was and Poulose stood there like a living corpse lost in prayer. A number of ugly looking figures appeared asking their leader to let them have Poulose for a meal. The leader counselled patience and suggested that they wait until he assessed Poulose's ability to live as one of them. He then called Poulose towards him and asked him who he was and how he happened to wander into their area. Speaking softly and affectionately he said, "If you are willing to live amicably among us you are welcome to stay. Your needs will all be taken care of. In any case our custom is not to let anyone leave us and those who do not live by our rules will be handed over to the cannibals among us."

Poulose decided that there was no alternative to agreeing to stay as he would then be able to escape immediate death. Thereafter by God's grace he might find a way out. So Poulose conveyed his decision to the leader who was happy with Poulose and his gentle, humble demeanour. He then assured Poulose of total safety and proceeded to give detailed advice on the rules binding the members of that community. "I am pleased with you and am accepting you as my disciple. I shall teach you all the forms of magic in which I am expert. We are a hill tribe and all of us have knowledge of magic but I am most skilled in it. Except for a few outsiders like you who serve us, all of us are from the same tribe. This cave is our abode but we do go out into the countryside and perform miracles. Nobody knows who we are or where we live. That is why we do not allow anybody to go out on their own. A few of our servants eat human flesh but will do nothing without my permission. If you are willing to stay here you may discard all your clothes as all those who live here have to go naked."

Poulose did not at all like the idea of nudity but he had no option. He lived there and commenced his lessons in various forms of magic. He did not enjoy living with the uncivilized, barbarian-like tribesmen but was provided with all comforts. Poulose lived thus for twelve years. In this period he became expert in all the magical skills and grew devoted to his teacher who, in turn, began to love him as a son. However, the desire to escape somehow was never far from Poulose's mind and the suspicion that Poulose might do exactly that was in the leader's thoughts. Therefore,

174

guards were posted day and night at the opening of the cave to watch over Poulose. It had also been agreed that the guards would call out to Poulose from time to time and that Poulose would respond. Although Poulose had the means to cast a spell over the guards and escape he did not have the heart to betray his teacher who had taught him these magical skills. Caught in this dilemma Poulose lost interest in food and sleep and began to show signs of despondency which were noticed by the leader. The latter called him to his side one day and asked him "Why are you looking so sad? Do you wish to leave us and go away?" Poulose replied, "What is the use? As long as you do not permit me to go I shall not be able to leave. I am also reluctant to leave you but at the same time I wish so much to see the priest who looked after me from my childhood. These thoughts make me very sad but I shall abide by your decision."

The leader replied, "I am so happy you spoke the truth. I am also reluctant to be separated from you but at the same time I have no desire to cause you grief. It is against our practice to release those who come here. If I deliberately let you go my followers will consider me to be mentally unsound and so I shall not order your release. I, however, permit you to act as you wish and I shall feign ignorance. If you are clever enough to dodge the guards you may make your escape. As you are so keen to see your guardian I am sure you will return to see me also." Poulose promised he could never forget the leader or cease to respect him. Poulose was then sworn to secrecy about the cave and its inhabitants.

That night he sought the blessings of his mentor, managed to retrieve his clothes and using his magical powers he put the guards under a spell and escaped from the cave. There was moonlight as he walked hastily away from the cave and in due course he saw several pathways in the dense forest but he did not know where they went. Finally he decided to take one of them in the hope that it would lead to some kind of habitation from where he could ask for help to find his way home. He knew that his spell over the guards would last only for a short while and feared that they would pursue him as soon as they came out of it. He put more speed into his walk and by dawn he saw some signs of human life. He was so overcome by hunger and fatigue that he entered a wayside hut in which he saw an old woman all by herself. He asked feebly for some food. The old woman replied, "My son, there was not even a grain of rice yesterday and so I have not been able to cook any food. I have to go and find some rice somewhere and if you are willing to wait I shall cook it and share it with you." Poulose asked her to see if there was even one grain of rice she could find and bring to him.

The old woman was convinced Poulose was mad but went to search for a grain of rice. This she found and handed over to Poulose. He asked her to boil some water which she did although she was certain that the man was mad. When the water was boiling Poulose put the grain of rice in it and very soon the old woman found that the pot was full of rice gruel. She was unable to believe her eyes and both of them had a hearty meal. Thus Poulose put to use yet another skill learnt from the caveman. Thereafter he ascertained that Katamattam was hardly four miles away and, greatly relieved, he dropped off into fatigued slumber.

In the morning he set out and finally reached the church where the priest could hardly recognize him. When Poulose identified himself the priest was overjoyed as Poulose had been given up as dead. Both shed tears of joy and when they had composed themselves Poulose related in carefully chosen words how he was kidnapped by bad men and held captive for years.

As they were engaged in conversation the caretaker of the church came racing in, bathed in perspiration and panting heavily. He cried out, "Our church has been taken over by evil spirits. They are fearful to look at and as tall as coconut trees. It is evening and time for the evening prayer but I dare not enter the church to ring the bell as they will eat me up alive. You have to decide whether to give up the evening prayer as in any case nobody will enter the church." Hearing this , Poulose rose and offered to go to the church with the caretaker and drive the evil spirits away. However, the priest would not let him go saying, "No, I shall go. I am eighty-eight years old and it does not matter if something happens to me. You are young and have years ahead of you."

Poulose assured the priest that God was with them and all three could go to the church. As they approached the church, Poulose knew that his fears were justified and that the evil ones were the cavemen who had pursued him. Poulose called out to them, "This is a place of worship and you have no place here. If you wish to stay alive you must leave this instant or you will be destroyed." To this the reply was, "We have come to get you and we shall only return with you." They came towards Poulose threateningly whereupon Poulose cast a spell on them and they dropped to the ground in a faint. The priest and the caretaker could not believe their eyes. The churchbell rang, people gathered for evening prayer as usual. After the prayer the people were full of praise for Poulose's magical skill. The priest was anxious that the ugly forms should be removed from the church. Poulose released the cavemen from his spell and they fled from the scene. The people gathered there were over-awed by Poulose's magical powers and the priest asked him how he came to acquire them. Poulose's reply was modest, "I have no powers. These are all by God's grace."

Very soon after this incident it was decided by the clergy that Poulose should enter full-fledged priesthood and he came to be known as "Kadamattathu Kathanaar" or the "Priest of Katamattam". He continued to live with his senior who was the vicar of the church.

Poulose became known for his power to overcome evil spirits and his services were in demand from far and near, for which he received good monetary rewards. He thus became prosperous and when the vicar died he moved into his own residence where he was able to engage servants.

The fame of "Katamattathu Kathanaar" was such that people began to believe that there was nothing that he could not achieve. Never did he refuse to assist those seeking help regardless of where he had to travel. Neither did he specify his price for his services and as a result he always received more than he expected. In course of time he became very wealthy indeed. Soon he began to impart his magical skills to students from all around and the Katamattathu system of training in magical skills became established. He kept his promise to his caveman mentor and not once till his death did he reveal the source of his knowledge. He wrote the story of his life on palmyra leaves and this was how the world came to know about him after his death.

With his death his family also disappeared and there is not even a trace of his house. However, many of those who practice magic still go to that location and sit in meditation and pray for success. It is relevant to take a look at some of the miracles performed by Katamattathu Kathanaar.

Long ago there was no road connecting Thiruvananthapuram (Trivandrum) with Padmanabhapuram and people who wished to travel between these places had to walk through dense forest. One day a witch decided to take up residence in the forest. She took the form of a very beautiful woman and began to accost the wayfarers, asking them for an ingredient to make up her betel leaf combination for chewing. Anyone who acceded to her request was persuaded by her with sweet words to go into the forest with her where she promptly drank his blood and then ate him up. The people tried every means including the use of reputed magicians to eliminate the witch but it was all in vain.

Finally the people sought the assistance of Kadamattathu Kathanaar who promptly entered the forest to be accosted by the witch in the form of a stunning beauty. As usual she asked for some lime for her betel leaf which the priest gave placed on an iron nail which she was reluctant to accept. Witches and evil spirits have an aversion to iron objects. When she eventually accepted the lime on the nail she became a captive of the priest. What she did not know was that the nail had really been driven into her head. From that moment the witch could do nothing other than follow the priest as he continued his journey through the forest. In about four days, after a few halts on the way, they reached Kayamkulam where the priest's aunt lived alone. The witch was introduced to the aunt by the priest as his servant. The aunt asked her nephew if the servant could stay with her as she was alone. The priest readily agreed and the witch was received into the household with great warmth. The two women prepared food and after dinner sat engaged in conversation while the priest went to sleep. The old lady treated the young woman as her child and insisted on combing the latter's hair. While doing this she found something obstructing the comb and found it was a nail. Without knowing what she was doing, she pulled out the nail and the witch was freed from the spell cast by the priest. She disappeared in a moment and the old lady ran to the priest to tell him of this strange happening.

The priest knew what had happened and set off in pursuit of the witch. He saw her in the distance and although he hurried to catch up with her she eluded him at the river by taking the only ferry available at that time. The priest, not to be outdone, immobilsed the witch through his magic, cut down a banana leaf and, using his magical power, crossed the river on that. He then approached the witch and warned her that unless she swore never to harm anybody he would cut her up and put her in a sacrificial fire. She swore never to harm anyone and as far as is known she kept her promise. However reports continued to come that on every New Moon, Fridays, and on certain other days she could be sighted at midnight as a beautiful woman.

Another story is about the friendship that existed between Kadamattathu Kathanaar and the head of the Kunjaman family of Nambudiris. The head of the family was himself skilled in magic and an undercurrent of rivalry existed between the two friends. The Nambudiri gloated over the fact that he had control over poltergeists who were evil spirits that indulged in mischief. In fact a few of these spirits were held as servants in the family. The priest prided himself on the wider range of magical powers which he had than the Nambudiri.

The Nambudiri used to travel in his rowing boat in which the oarsmen were the evil spirits under his control and as they were invisible it appeared as if the boat was moving on its own. The priest decided to visit his friend and, using his magical power, moved his boat without any visible means of propulsion. On hearing that a boat had come close to his house without any motive power, the Nambudiri came out to investigate. He asked the priest how he managed to move the boat without oarsmen and the priest replied, "I decided to visit you but then found that no oarsmen were available. I asked the boat to bring me here and so here I am." The Nambudiri saw through this plan but said nothing.

The priest was invited to the Nambudiri's home and treated with much hospitality. They sat in conversation for a long time when the priest said he had to leave as it was getting late. The Nambudiri was insistent that his friend should stay for a few days but the priest had to leave in order to keep an appointment in Changanacherry. Both of them went to the riverside but the priest's boat was missing. They looked around and found that the boat was resting in the branches of a mango tree near by. The priest knew that his friend had deliberately had this mischief done through the poltergeists. He asked the Nambudiri to bring the boat down but the latter pleaded his inability to do so. The priest then said, "I know that you have done this. If you do not bring the boat back I shall see that the womenfolk in your family come out naked and bring the boat down for me." The Nambudiri challenged the priest who resorted to his magic. Very soon the Nambudiri saw the women of his family emerging from his house without any clothes and realised he could not match the priest's powers. He appealed to the priest to withdraw his spell and promised never to compete with his friend. He had the boat brought down, the spell was withdrawn, and the friendship continued into the following years.

There was the time that a leader of the church arrived in Kerala from Jerusalem or somewhere. He happened to visit the church in Kadamattam where he was received by the priest with honours and various offerings. The visitor was taken by surprise as most of the offerings were known not to be available outside Europe. He remarked that fresh grapes also could have been included among the offerings as he was sure these could also be available in plenty. The priest assured his guest that this was true and that one grape put in the soil would instantly produce bunches of grapes. Saying this he put one grape into the ground and within moments grape vines appeared laden with bunches of grapes. The visitor found that these grapes looked and tasted exactly like real grapes.

While leaving the church one of the bystanders informed the visiting priest that his host was skilled in magic and that the grapes were a product of this magic. He also added that the priest's residence stored many scripts detailing the art of magic. The visitor went to his host's residence, collected all these scripts, and set them alight. The scripts immediately turned into birds and flew away into the sky suffering no damage from the fire. The visiting leader then summoned the priest and advised him against the use of magical powers as they were considered inappropriate in their religion. The priest pleaded with his senior visitor to be allowed the use of his skills as they were utilized only to help and never to harm. This permission was finally granted after much debate.

On another occasion the ruler of Cochin sought the priest's help to rid his state of harassment by alien forces. The priest handed the ruler an arrow over which special prayers had been said and suggested that it be fired into the alien camp. The moment this was done the aliens started fighting among themselves in a demented state and destroyed themselves!

There is no end to the stories about the miracles performed by Katamattathu Kathanaar, the Priest of Katamattam.

Two Royal Personalities*

*A short-tempered but good-hearted ruler and
a queen endowed with divinity.*

The last ruler of Chempakasseri or Ambalapuzha in Travancore
was a short-tempered but good-hearted man. It was during his
reign that the Maharaja Marthanda Varma annexed that territory to
Travancore State.

Marthanda Varma once sent a letter to the Chempakasseri ruler
saying, "I wish to know the quality of your soil. When do I have to
come for this purpose?" The Chempakasseri ruler gave this letter to
his minister Mathur Panikkar to send an appropriate reply. The reply
went as follows: "A basket and some money may be sent here through a
messenger. The sample will be sent back and there is no need for a visit
by Your Highness." Both messages carried hidden meanings. Marthanda
Varma had suggested that he wished to take over Ambalapuzha and the
reply in turn refused to give in to the threat.

Marthanda Varma was very impressed by the reply and Panikkar's
courage. He wrote again to the Chempakasseri ruler complimenting
Panikkar's courage and expressing a desire to meet him. The ruler
discussed the matter with Panikkar and expressed his fear that this
could be a ruse to take Panikkar captive. Panikkar, however, discounted
this fear and said a refusal to go could be taken to be cowardice. He
offered to go and meet Marthanda Varma.

Marthanda Varma gave Panikkar an audience on arrival and
rewarded him with honours such as golden bracelets. One is unable to
tell whether this was because the Maharaja discovered that Panikkar
could not be threatened and that persuasion could be a better option.
The Chempakasseri ruler was very pleased to see his minister return
with honours but there were Panikkar's enemies who whispered into
the ruler's ears that Panikkar had been rewarded for secretly agreeing to
help Marthanda Varma annex Chempakasseri. In a fit of rage the ruler

---
Chembakasseri Raajaavum Rajniyum

ordered Panikkar bound and executed. It is obvious that the order to execute a loyal, patriotic, and honest citizen could only have been the act of an unthinking man consumed by uncontrollable anger.

The womenfolk of the Chempakasseri family lived in Kutamalur and the rulers often visited Kutamalur. On one occasion the short-tempered Chempakasseri ruler was in Kutamalur when a cow strayed into a Muslim's property. The Muslim threw a stone at the cow which collapsed. The owner of the cow ran to the ruler complaining that the Muslim had killed his cow. The ruler was enraged and had the Muslim hanged. The cow recovered from the blow after a while and strolled away. When this news reached the ruler there was nothing he could do but curse the owner of the cow and his family with ruin for having an innocent man killed. The good heart of the ruler and the sincerity of his curse are said to have brought ruin to the owner of the cow and his family.

There was once a senior princess of the Ambalapuzha royal family who was enlightened and very pious. It was believed that even the gods and goddesses listened to her. Near her palace on the southern bank of the river Kounar was a temple in which the deity was a powerful incarnation of Kali. The deity originally faced north and it so happened that boats passing the temple along the river at night sank without reason and soon all boat traffic stopped.

The princess came to hear about this and decided that the situation had to be remedied. She visited the temple and addressed the deity, "Oh Devi, thanks to your line of sight over the river all traffic has stopped. This is sad and I pray you face east instead of north." At dawn the next day it was seen that the deity was facing east. Traffic was restored and all was well again.

The cowshed of the Kutamalur palace was where the princess went at dawn every day to view the cows for an auspicious start of the day. While she did this she prayed to the deity of the Guruvayur temple, Lord Krishna. Early one morning when she went as usual to the cowshed she saw Lord Krishna in his childhood form playing in the cowshed. She immediately prostrated before this form which disappeared when she opened her eyes. She ordered that a Krishna temple be built at that site and she continued to visit that temple. This is the origin of the now famous Kutamalur temple.

Through Faith to Fame*

Strong faith in the family deity was a chracteristic of the families in the old days and this is one of the many stories of how this helped them overcome adversity.

The Pilamanthol family is located in Valluvanad taluk in what was British Malabar but is now in North Kerala. The family has been renowned for its tradition and wealth of successful practitioners of indigenous medicine.

Long ago the then Maharaja of Travancore had a serious stomach ailment which defied the treatment of all the known doctors who were summoned. It was then decided that a Pilamanthol Moos should be invited to treat the Maharaja and messengers were sent to Pilamanthol for this purpose. Unfortunately the Pilamanthol family was in a strange situation in which it did not have a single male adult and the only male was a fourteen year old who had no knowledge of medicine whatsoever. The royal messengers met this young lad and conveyed their message which left the young Moos terribly despondent. He was deeply pained that his father had died too early to pass on to him the traditional knowledge of the family. As a result the family was in the humiliating position of not being able to respond to the royal summons, virtually betraying the trust everybody including the Maharaja had in the expertise of the family. He finally went to his mother and poured out his agony to her. The mother consoled him and said, "Do not worry. Our family deity Lord Shiva will find a way for us. You should worship in the family temple for twelve days and you may now tell the messengers that you will be available after twelve days." This message was conveyed to the messengers who then preferred to stay back and return home with the young man after twelve days.

The young Moos commenced his stay in the temple and spent all his time praying to Lord Shiva. Before twelve days had passed, one night,

---

*Pilamanthol Moos

he had a vision of an old Brahmin who reassured him with these words, "There is no cause for anxiety. Please go to Travancore and give these three tablets to the Maharaja to be taken three times in warm water. He will be cured. Please do not accept any reward that the Maharaja may give you. He will ask you what you wish to have. You are then to request the Maharaja to retrieve the idol of Dhanvanthari (patron deity of medicine) from the river Thamraparni and establish it on the left side of your family deity, Lord Shiva, in the same temple. When the Maharaja's men go to the banks of the river there will be somebody there to guide them to the spot in the river where the idol lies." Moos woke up and looked for the visitor but all he found were three tablets in his hand.

After seeking his mother's blessings a day after completing his worship, Moos left for Travancore with the Maharaja's men. He visited the Maharaja and prescribed the tablets which he handed over. The Maharaja made a miraculous recovery and offered Moos generous rewards which Moos refused to accept. The ruler asked how he would like to be rewarded. Moos responded as advised in the vision and the Maharaja duly sent his men to the shores of Thamraparni river to retrieve the idol. As they were standing on the river bank a saintly looking man approached them and pointed to an eagle flying overhead. He directed them to search right below where the eagle was flying and that was where they found the idol. The saint asked them to take it to Pilamanthol and make preparations for establishing the idol in the Shiva temple. He said he would arrive there in time to perform the rituals for this. The idol was taken to Pilamanthol, bathed in the local river, and set up there temporarily while a new sanctum sanctorum was built on the left side of the Shiva idol in the family temple. As the hour for consecrating the new temple approached, the saint appeared and asked that the idol be brought. Two Brahmins went to fetch the idol but as they could not lift it many more were sent but they too failed. Finally the saint went to the river, lifted the idol with one hand and brought it to the temple. The rituals were performed and the Pilamanthol family thereafter treated both Shiva and Dhanvanthari as the family deities. Both deities were treated identically and all offerings were made to both in exactly the same manner.

The young Moos trained in medicine under a very famous practitioner, Alathur Nambi, and eventually became famous in his own right. He married one of Nambi's daughters and had many sons all of whom over the years were able to maintain the glorious family tradition in medical practice.

The saint who presided over the consecration of the new temple stayed on in the temple for years and when he died his body was laid to rest between the two temples. A sacred tulsi plant can still be seen at that spot.

A few generations later the Pilamanthol family dwindled to just one young woman. At that time the Zamorin (ruler) of Calicut (now Kozhikode) suffered from a serious diabetic ulcer on his back and in the absence of a Pilamanthol doctor, was treated by a Nambudiri who was a disciple of one of the Pilamanthol practitioners. The treatment included surgery which was also performed by the Nambudiri. This was objected to by the other Nambudiris who began to harass the doctor so much that he found it difficult to live in his own house. He sought the Zamorin's help and the Zamorin arranged for him to marry the young woman from the Pilamanthol family. The Zamorin also presented them with land and other assets which are still enjoyed by the succeeding generations, the present one of which consists of a father, mother, two sons and a daughter. It is to be hoped that with God's grace, the family will flourish.

The Invisible Family

A magically gifted man has a daughter by a divine spirit, an event commemorated even today by a religious festival.

It was the custom in the Nambudiri family of Vayaskara that whenever the family was reduced to a single young woman a member of one of the other noted families married into Vayaskara and thereafter had Vayaskara prefixed to his surname. There was thus a Vayaskara Moos, a Vayaskara Bhattathiri and so on.

Once upon a time there was a Vayaskara Bhattathiri who was very learned in the four Vedas and was known as Chaturvedi (*chatur* – four, *vedi* – one learned in Vedas) Bhattathiri. Besides his knowledge of scriptures he was an expert in indigenous medicine and also possessed magical powers. The magical powers kept him in great demand from all around that area.

During that time the Zamorin of Calicut (now Kozhikode) was possessed by a yakshi (a female spirit who attends on gods and goddesses). All attempts by various experts in sorcery failed to release the Zamorin from the yakshi. Chaturvedi Bhattathiri was summoned and he used his power over spirits to free the Zamorin who rewarded Bhattathiri generously and sent him on his way.

On his return from Calicut it was getting dark and Bhattathiri decided to spend the night in a Nambudiri household on the way. He had his bath and dinner and tired as he was from his journey, promptly fell asleep. He then heard someone telling him, "Please remove that packet from under your pillow." Bhattathiri opened his eyes and saw a very beautiful woman standing beside him. He could see her clearly in the light of the lamp that was still burning. It was Bhattathiri's practice to carry with him a small bundle of palmyra leaves on which were written his magical verses. This was a precaution he took in the light of his practice which put him in conflict with various kinds of spirits.

---

*Vayaskara Chaturvedi Bhattathiriyum Yakshiyum

Bhattathiri questioned her about her identity and she turned out to be the spirit who had been troubling the Zamorin. She said, "I have fallen in love with you. I cannot approach you until those palmyra leaves are removed." Bhattathiri extracted a promise from her that he would not be harmed and then removed the palmyra leaves. She joined him in bed and, needless to say, they had an enjoyable night together.

Dawn came and the yakshi insisted on going with Bhattathiri who happily agreed to take her with him. They travelled together and she was invisible to all eyes except Bhattathiri's. They reached Vayaskara and continued to live as husband and wife without anyone else knowing it. Soon thereafter the yakshi gave birth to a girl after which the yakshi left the daughter with the father and disappeared. The daughter was also invisible to all human eyes except her father's.

Years rolled by and Bhattathiri knew his end was near. He called his daughter and asked her to stay on in the family as its deity and be worshipped and revered as such. He then called his eldest son by his real wife and explained to him all that had happened between him and the yakshi. He then said that the young yakshi should be worshipped as the family deity and instructed his son on the rituals to be observed.

It is believed that the young yakshi continues to live in the Vayaskara home. Until some years ago people used to claim having seen her in different forms – as a beautiful woman, as a ball of fire, etc. An annual festival is conducted even to this day in Vayaskara in which the forms of Bhattathiri and the yakshi are drawn on the ground using powders of five colours and the rituals include singing of prayers one of which refers to the yakshi as Bhattathiri's daughter. In the light of these one has to assume that the story is not entirely without truth.

Glossary

appam : A cup-shaped, deep-fried Kerala sweet made from wheat flour, coconut, jaggery, etc., popular in temples as an offering.

Ashtavaidya : Eight (ashta) families of renowned Ayurvedic physicians (vaidyas).

Bhattathiri, Moos, Nambudiri : Categories of Kerala Brahmins, the difference among them reflecting the levels of their attainments in the study of religious rituals and Sanskrit scriptures.

Chakyar / Chakyar Koothu : *Chakyar Koothu* is an art form traditionally performed only in temples. This was the privilege of a small community of Chakyars who performed koothu in special colourful costumes, made-up face, and accompanied by a *mizhavu,* a percussion instrument made out of a huge earthen jar with its small mouth closed with hide, and *elathalam*, small cymbals. The Chakyar recites stories from mythology in Sanskrit verse and in explaining the content draws from contemporary issues to hold audience interest. Rulers, the nobility and persons in positions of authority are always part of the audience and the Chakyar often addresses them with barbs and jibes relating to local problems. Tradition forbids any response from the audience.

Dewan : The Prime Minister of the erstwhile princely States of India that were merged after Independence with the provinces under Central administration.

Elaya Raja : "Younger Raja", the heir apparent in the erstwhile princely States of Kerala.

guru : Teacher or mentor.

musth : The mating period of male elephants during which elephants in captivity have to be restrained by chains for two months or so as they turn violent. A watery liquid with a characteristic odour flows from the side of the head during these months.

purdah : The traditional veil or screen used by Muslim women.

pariah : The lowest of the low in the Indian social hierarchy, they have no place in the caste system, also referred to as "untouchables".

Pooram festival : A festival held every year in May in Thrissur in Kerala, famous for the participation of two popular local temples, each fielding fifteen richly-caparisoned elephants and competing keenly with displays of vividly coloured, multi-tiered silken umbrellas switched by the minute and brilliant, noisy fireworks.

rudraksha : The berries of an Indian tree considered to be sacred. The berries are strung together and worn round the neck by devotees of Lord Shiva and ascetics, both men and women.

Shakthi : An incarnation of Goddess Bhagavathi whose worship permits the use of meat and alchohol.

Shudra : The lowest of the four "varnas" or caste groups in India.

Tahsildar : Head of a tahsil which forms part of a revenue district in the Indian administrative system.

taluk : A part of a revenue district similar to a tahsil.

Thangal : An honorific held by certain leaders of Muslim communities in Kerala.

tulsi : A sacred plant of India not unlike the western herb "basil".

Vedanta : The conclusion, goal of the Vedas which foregrounds the intellectuality of monism.

Zamorin : Also known locally as "Samoothiri", formerly the ruler of Kozhikode, which was known as Calicut.

About the Author

Kottarathil Sankunni (1855–1937) was Vasudevan Unni's pen name. Though Sankunni had no formal schooling, he was a scholar of Sanskrit classics and ayurvedic treatises. He knew enough English to tutor many European missionaries in Malayalam, which led to his appointment as the Malayalam *munshi* at the MD Seminary School at Kottayam.

This was where he met Kandathil Varughese Mappillai, who was the manager of the school, and who went on to become the founder-editor of *Malayala Manorama*. It was on his invitation that Sankunni joined the newspaper as its first poetry editor.

Sankunni was a prolific writer who contributed to a variety of genres of literature. He wrote thirteen *manipravalakritis*, translated three Sanskrit plays, mythological stories, some short stories, and songs written for specific kinds of dances and performances like *kaikothikali*, *kilipattu*, *thullalpaattukkal*, and *vanchi paattukkal*, and also contributed to prosody.

No poet was more recognized or rewarded than Kottarathil Sankunni by the royal houses of Thiruvananthapuram and Kochi, as also by the British rulers of the time.

About the Translator

T.C. Narayan studied in Madras and Ernakulam before embarking on a successful corporate career in India and abroad. He was an active participant and All India Radio commntator in competitive cricket, sailing, and tennis. Narayan was also visiting lecturer at the Staff Training College, Hyderabad, as well as at other corporate training centres.

Narayan has published a biography of a time gone by called *Ettukettu Stories* and has translated extended excerpts from *A Midsummer Night's Dream* into Malayalam, which were used by a travelling RADA performance sponsored by the British Council in 2006. Two more of Narayan's books will be published shortly.